Virginia SOL Grade 8 Reading

SECRETS

Study Guide
Your Key to Exam Success

Virginia SOL Test Review for the
Virginia Standards of Learning Examination

Dear Future Exam Success Story:

Congratulations on your purchase of our study guide. Our goal in writing our study guide was to cover the content on the test, as well as provide insight into typical test taking mistakes and how to overcome them.

Standardized tests are a key component of being successful, which only increases the importance of doing well in the high-pressure high-stakes environment of test day. How well you do on this test will have a significant impact on your future, and we have the research and practical advice to help you execute on test day.

The product you're reading now is designed to exploit weaknesses in the test itself, and help you avoid the most common errors test takers frequently make.

How to use this study guide

We don't want to waste your time. Our study guide is fast-paced and fluff-free. We suggest going through it a number of times, as repetition is an important part of learning new information and concepts.

First, read through the study guide completely to get a feel for the content and organization. Read the general success strategies first, and then proceed to the content sections. Each tip has been carefully selected for its effectiveness.

Second, read through the study guide again, and take notes in the margins and highlight those sections where you may have a particular weakness.

Finally, bring the manual with you on test day and study it before the exam begins.

Your success is our success

We would be delighted to hear about your success. Send us an email and tell us your story. Thanks for your business and we wish you continued success.

Sincerely,

Mometrix Test Preparation Team

Need more help? Check out our flashcards at: http://MometrixFlashcards.com/SOL

TABLE OF CONTENTS

Top 20 Test Taking Tips

1. Carefully follow all the test registration procedures
2. Know the test directions, duration, topics, question types, how many questions
3. Setup a flexible study schedule at least 3-4 weeks before test day
4. Study during the time of day you are most alert, relaxed, and stress free
5. Maximize your learning style; visual learner use visual study aids, auditory learner use auditory study aids
6. Focus on your weakest knowledge base
7. Find a study partner to review with and help clarify questions
8. Practice, practice, practice
9. Get a good night's sleep; don't try to cram the night before the test
10. Eat a well balanced meal
11. Know the exact physical location of the testing site; drive the route to the site prior to test day
12. Bring a set of ear plugs; the testing center could be noisy
13. Wear comfortable, loose fitting, layered clothing to the testing center; prepare for it to be either cold or hot during the test
14. Bring at least 2 current forms of ID to the testing center
15. Arrive to the test early; be prepared to wait and be patient
16. Eliminate the obviously wrong answer choices, then guess the first remaining choice
17. Pace yourself; don't rush, but keep working and move on if you get stuck
18. Maintain a positive attitude even if the test is going poorly
19. Keep your first answer unless you are positive it is wrong
20. Check your work, don't make a careless mistake

Reading Assessment

Prefix, suffix, and root word

Root word: The base part of a compound word when one takes away any prefixes or suffixes. The root carries the base meaning that the prefix or suffix alters.

Prefix: A part of a word that is added onto the front of a root word and cannot stand alone. It does have its own meaning, so it changes or enhances the meaning of the root word to make a new word. For example, the prefix *un-* changes the meaning of the root *happy* when it is added: *un*happy means *not* happy.

Suffix: A part of a word that is added onto the end of a root word and, like a prefix, cannot stand alone. It also has its own meaning so it changes or enhances the meaning of the root word to make a new word. For example, the suffix *-ness* changes the meaning of the root *happy:* happi*ness* means *the state of* being happy.

Knowledge of prefixes and suffixes can help one determine the meaning of an unfamiliar word by helping to break the word down into all of its parts: prefix + root word + suffix. Look first at the individual meanings of the root word, prefix and/or suffix. Using knowledge of the meaning(s) of the prefix and/or suffix to see what information it adds to the root. Even if the meaning of the root is unknown, one can use knowledge of the prefix's and/or suffix's meaning(s) to determine an approximate meaning of the word. For example, if one sees the word *uninspired* and does not know what it means, they can use the knowledge that *un-* means 'not' to know that the full word means "not inspired."

Examples
The word orthography can be broken down into the following parts: ortho + graph + y. The prefix of the word is ortho-, meaning 'straight' or 'correct'. The root of the word is graph, which means 'write', 'draw', or 'written'. The suffix of the word is -y, which changes the word to a noun when added to the end of it, and means 'state' or 'condition'. Using this knowledge, an approximate definition of the word orthography would be "the state of being written correctly." The dictionary definition of the word orthography is "writing words using the proper letters." The approximate definition taken from the parts can often be close to the true definition.

The word *geometric* can be broken down into the following parts: geo + metri + ic. The prefix of the word is *geo-*, meaning 'earth'. The root of the word is *metri-* (similar in meaning to the root *meter-*), which means 'measure'. The suffix of the word is *-ic,* meaning 'having to do with'. Using this knowledge, an approximate definition of the word *geometric* would be "having to do with measuring the earth." The dictionary definition of the word *geometric* is "of or relating to the branch of mathematics that has to do with measuring points, lines, and angles."

<u>Common prefixes</u>

The following is a list of commonly used prefixes:

- *anti-* : opposite. Example word: antiwar.
- *auto-*: self. Example word: autograph.
- *bi-*: two. Example word: bicycle.
- *bio-*: life, living. Example word: biology.
- *circum-*: around. Example word: circumference.
- *con-, com-*: with, together. Example words: construct, combine.
- *de-*: from, down, away. Example word: derail.
- *dis-*: not, negative. Example word: disregard.
- *in-, im-*: not. Example words: inequality, impossible.
- *inter-*: between. Example word: international.
- *mis-*: bad, badly. Example word: misunderstand.
- *non-*: not. Example word: nonsense.
- *re-*: back, again. Example word: react.
- *sub-*: under, below. Example word: submarine.
- *un-*: not. Example word: unhappy.

<u>Common suffixes</u>

The following is a list of commonly used suffixes:

- *-able, -ible*: capable of. Example words: available, invisible.
- *-ance, -ence*: quality or process. Example words: resistance, independence.
- *-er, -or*: person who. Example words: writer, contactor.
- *-ful*: full of. Example word: thoughtful.
- *-ion, -tion*: condition or action. Example words: narration, evolution.
- *-ism*: belief. Example word: socialism.
- *-ist*: person or member. Example word: internist.
- *-ment*: condition. Example word: enjoyment.
- *-nes* : state or condition. Example word: emptiness.
- *-ship*: state of being connected. Example word: relationship.
- *-y*: state or condition. Example word: windy.

Multiple meaning words

Some words are spelled exactly the same but have different meanings in different contexts. One needs to use the context of the situation to determine the correct meaning of the word. These words can be used as either a noun or a verb and their grammatical usage determines the meaning. The word *trip* could be either a noun or a verb. *Trip* as a noun means 'vacation', where *trip* as a verb means to fall over something.

Here are two different sentences using *trip* as a noun and a verb:

> Last year, she went on an amazing *trip* to Santa Fe, New Mexico, with her sister.

> If you aren't watching where you are going, you might *trip* over a bump in the cement.

The word *degree* has at least three different meanings, depending on the situation in which the word is used: (a) a *degree* is the incremental measurement of temperature; (b) a *degree* is a title awarded upon graduation from college; and (c) *degree* can mean the extent or amount of something.

Here are three different sentences, each using one of these meanings of the word *degree*:

> You probably don't notice a difference when the temperature rises one *degree*.

> The employer is only willing to hire someone with a *degree* in mathematics.

> It was hard to tell the *degree* to which he really cared about the outcome.

Denotation and connotation

Denotation is the literal meaning, or dictionary definition, of a word and is a completely objective meaning. Connotation is the meaning of a word as it is derived from the literal meaning <u>plus</u> the emotions or thoughts that one has about the word based on experiences, memories, feelings, and ideas. The connotation of a word is subjective, depending upon the thoughts and feelings of the reader and the situation in which the word is used. The words 'cheap' and 'inexpensive' both have the same denotative meaning of "not costing a lot of money." The word 'cheap', however, has the connotation of being "of low quality" whereas the word 'inexpensive' does not have that. Another example is the word *rat*. The denotative meaning of the word *rat* is a long-tailed rodent. Many people have strong emotions associated with rats so the connotative meaning may include views such as dirty, sleazy, and disgusting. Using the connotative meaning, one could call a sleazy person a rat even though he or she is not a long-tailed rodent.

Here are two different sentences using the denotative and connotative meaning of the word *snake*:

> One of the largest types of snake is the boa constrictor.

> If he weren't such a snake, we could rely on him to tell the truth.

The word *snake* has both a denotative and connotative meaning. In the first sentence, the word *snake* is used literally, as a reptile without legs. In the second sentence, the word *snake* is not used to refer to a reptile, but rather a person. This is how one knows that the connotative meaning of the word is being used. One can then use the context of the sentence to determine the connotative meaning of the word: in this case, a crafty, unreliable person.

Universal themes in literature

The theme of a piece of literature is its controlling idea. Universal themes are themes that can be discussed in regard to all of humanity. People all over the world can relate to stories that center on the struggle of man versus man, for example. Other universal themes include man versus nature, man versus himself, good versus evil, fate versus free will, triumph over adversity, and coming of age. Determine the theme of the following short paragraph:

Matt had spent a lot of time preparing for his first babysitting experience. Matt stayed fully attentive to his young cousin, Toby, while he played outside. When his aunt returned, Matt was proud to report that all had gone well. He had acted in the adult role.

The theme of a piece of literature is its controlling idea. The short paragraph shown here is a coming of age story. This means that the protagonist goes through some kind of experience that changes him or her from a child into an adult. By preparing to care for his cousin Toby and keeping him safe while his aunt was away, Matt became more of an adult and less of a child. Taking care of someone else is an adult thing to do and Matt was successful. This was a defining moment in his life.

Purpose

The four purposes of texts are: to inform, to influence or persuade, to express, and to entertain. Newspaper articles, encyclopedia entries, and functional documents are written to inform; authors give facts and write in an objective tone. Editorials and advertisements are written to influence; authors use persuasive language to try to be convincing. Descriptive paragraphs are written to express something; authors use lots of adjectives to describe objects. Fictional stories and screenplays are written to entertain; authors may use humor or dramatic elements to entertain their audiences.

Example 1
Gorillas are large primates. They live on the ground in the forests of Africa.

The sentences shown here contain factual information about gorillas. The author is not trying to describe the physical appearance of a gorilla or a situation in which a gorilla is doing something interesting. He is not trying to persuade the reader to do anything with regard to gorillas. He is not telling a story about gorillas. Thus, from this deduction, one can determine that the author is writing with the purpose of informing the reader about the gorilla and its habitat.

Example 2
Softsuds is the best shampoo on the market. It will leave your hair tangle-free and shiny. Try it out to see for yourself. Pick some up today.

There are four main purposes an author may have when writing: to inform, to express, to influence, and to entertain. The sentences shown here contain persuasive language about a certain brand of shampoo. The sentences might be used in a commercial or other advertisement. The author is not trying to give factual information about the shampoo. He is not trying to describe the aroma or feeling of the shampoo's lather. The author is not telling a story about an experience using the shampoo either. Thus, from this deduction, one can determine that the author is writing with the purpose of influencing or persuading the reader to use the Softsuds brand of shampoo.

Different perspective from different authors

An author tells a story from his or her own perspective. Different people have different perspectives, so they may tell the same story differently, emphasizing different aspects relative to their views. A prime example of this is a situation in which two people get into an argument. One person may blame the other for something and the second person may not see himself at fault, but rather think that his friend did something wrong first. It is for this reason that we have the expression, "to stand in someone else's shoes." In this way, the same situation may be explained or described differently by two different authors.

Comparison of communication in different forms

Some elements to include in a comparison of communication in different forms include aspects of the plot, characterization, and the author's use of language. If one has ever read a story and seen a movie of the same story, it is obvious that the director of the movie will often leave out certain scenes from the book that may not be easily depicted visually. This may change the flow of the story line or emphasize one strand of the plot over another. In addition, characterization may be different in different versions of the same story. Using dialogue differently and shifting the point of view may alter characterization across different forms of communication.

The use of figurative language may not be transferred verbatim when a dramatic performance is made based on a print version of a story either. Lastly, a dramatic performance, by its nature, includes a visual element that is lacking in a print story.

Venn diagram for comparison/contrast

A Venn diagram is a graphic organizer composed of two (or more) interlocking circles. It is best used to represent information where two items are being compared and contrasted. Facts and details about one item can be written in one circle (i.e., the green area on the left in the diagram below) and facts and details about the second item are written in the second circle (i.e., the purple area on the right in the diagram below). In the overlapping space of the two circles (i.e., the middle portion in the diagram below), facts and details that are true of both items are written. In this way, it is easy to see the similarities and differences between two (or more) things.

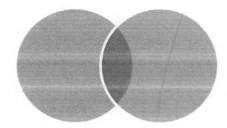

Epic poetry and lyric poetry

An epic poem is a lengthy, narrative poem that usually tells a story about a serious or heroic deed. These types of poems are important within specific cultures or groups of people. In an epic, the hero tends to go on a journey or a quest. The hero meets many adversaries and enemies along the way. Through each encounter the hero may learn something new. When the hero returns home he has changed significantly through his journey. Most often the hero's trials are related to morals that were important to the specific culture.

Lyric poetry is a type of poetry that expresses the author's personal feelings. This type of poetry is almost always emotional. They author will use sensory language to influence the audience's emotions. Originally, lyric poetry was written to be sung along with a lyre, a type of stringed instrument. It is a type of poetry that doesn't have to rhyme or even be set to music.

Style, tone, and mood

Authors use language and word choice to convey a certain style, tone, and mood in a piece of literature. When an author writes, he or she uses a style appropriate to the purpose of the text, but also uses language in a way that sets him or her apart. Tone is the author's attitude toward the subject and mood is the feeling the work invokes in the reader. Authors use their own personal style, their attitude toward the subject, and the mood they create to help craft their stories. Style, tone, and mood all contribute to the effect of a text. As readers, we know there is a difference between a serious or humorous piece, for example.

Plot line

Every plot line follows the same stages. One can identify each of these stages in every story they read. These stages are: the introduction, rising action, conflict, climax, falling action, and resolution. The introduction tells the reader what the story will be about and sets up the plot. The rising action is what happens that leads up to the conflict, which is some sort of problem that arises, with the climax at its peak. The falling action is what happens after the climax of the conflict. The resolution is the conclusion and often has the final solution to the problem in the conflict.

A plot line looks like this:

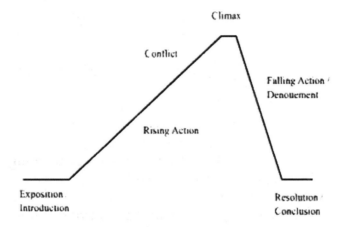

Common characteristics in literature

Some common characteristics found in all genres of literary text, from historical fiction to fables, include character, plot, conflict/resolution, and setting. The characters are the people who do the action in the story. The plot is the storyline and generally includes a conflict, or problem, and its resolution, or the way that the main character solves the problem in the story. The setting is the time and place where the story takes place.

Character analysis

When one analyzes a character, one should pay attention to the character's physical traits, thoughts, feelings and attitudes, and motivations. Physical traits include any description of how the character appears, for example, this can include hair and eye color, height, and clothing. The character's thoughts, feelings, and attitudes include his or her ideas about certain topics or other characters in the story. The character's

- 8 -

motivations are the reasons why he or she behaves a certain way. For example, in a mystery novel, the protagonist may act in a deceitful way toward a suspect but the motivation for doing so may be to gain information and uncover the truth. This lets the reader understand that even though the character acts in a deceitful way, he or she is not a bad person. The motivation allows the reader to better understand the character and their actions.

Point of view

The point of view of a text is the perspective from which it is told. Every literary text has a narrator, or person who tells the story. The two main points of view that authors use are first person and third person. If the narrator is also the main character, or protagonist, of a work, it is written in first person point of view. In first person, the author writes with the word, "I" and gives the reader insights into all of their thoughts and opinions. Third person point of view is probably the most common. Using third person, authors refer to each character using "he" or "she." In third person omniscient, the narrator is not a character in the story and can tell the story of all of the characters at the same time, often revealing their thoughts and opinions as they become relevant.

Authors' choose which point of view they want to use in their text in order to best achieve their purpose. For example, using first person point of view can make a story seem more intimate, but the reader only sees the story line from the perspective of the narrator. If a writer wants the reader to understand the motivations of more than one character, he or she would use third person omniscient narrative. This is an overall narrative where the reader sees everything happening in the story, often with insights into multiple characters' minds.

When a story is written from the first person point of view, it is told from the point of view of the narrator, who is often the main character, or protagonist. The story is told using the pronouns "I" and "me." When a story is told from one character's point of view, the scope is limited to what that character thinks and knows and the story carries that character's biases; it is not a broad telling of the story from an outside and objective narrator. Regardless, an author might choose to use first person point of view because it can be very intimate. The reader feels very close to the protagonist and understands the situation from his or her perspective.

Example
Read the following excerpt from Jane Austen's Emma and discuss the point of view:

"Doing just what she liked; highly esteeming Miss Taylor's judgments, but directed chiefly by her own. The real evils, indeed, of Emma's situation were the power of having rather too much her own way, and a disposition to think a little too well of herself."

In order to determine the point of view, one should first look at the pronouns used in the passage. If the passage has the pronoun "I" it is probably written in first person point of view, in which the protagonist is the narrator. In the case of this excerpt, a narrator who is not the protagonist is telling the story. The pronouns used are "she" and "her" which are clues that someone is talking about the character rather than the character speaking for herself, indicating it is written in the third person point of view. An outside narrator is telling the story *about* Emma, she is not telling the story about herself.

Inference

An inference is a conclusion that the reader makes using clues in the text. In a fictional work of literature, there are things that the author does not explicitly mention, but hints at; the reader needs to connect the dots of these clues to draw a conclusion. This is called making an inference. An inference is different from making a guess, as an inference is based on evidence; the reader needs to use specific textual evidence to make the inference. For example, an author might mention that a character has a messy room and papers falling out of his binder. The reader can infer that the character is sloppy and disorganized even though the author does not explicitly state this fact.

<u>Examples</u>
An inference can be made about the character of the narrator based on the following excerpt from <u>David Copperfield</u> by Charles Dickens:

My father's eyes had closed upon the light of this world six months, when mine opened on it. There is something strange to me...in the shadowy remembrance that I have of my first childish associations with his white grave-stone in the churchyard, and of the indefinable compassion I used to feel for it lying out alone there in the dark night, when our little parlour was warm and bright with fire and candle, and the doors of our house were - almost cruelly, it seemed to me sometimes - bolted and locked against it.

In order to make an inference, the reader must use clues from the passage to come to a conclusion. It is explicitly stated in the passage that David's father died before he was born. Based on the excerpt, the reader can infer that David Copperfield feels sadness over the loss of his father, even though he never knew him. This inference about David's character can be made using context clues from the passage: David feels "indefinable compassion" for his father's gravestone. The phrase "almost cruelly" indicates that David feels that his family is perhaps too harsh in their treatment of his father. He feels a connection to his father's gravestone and feels bad that the stone is left out in the cold when his house is warm.

An inference can be made about the character Pip based on the following excerpt from <u>Great Expectations</u> by Charles Dickens:

- 10 -

I never had one hour's happiness in her society, and yet my mind all round the four-and-twenty hours was harping on the happiness of having her with me unto death.

In order to make an inference, the reader must use clues from the passage to come to a conclusion. This excerpt shows the reader Pip, who is thinking about a romantic relationship with a woman. The words "yet my mind all round the four and twenty hours" and "harping" lead the reader to infer that he has a crush on this woman and cannot get her out of his thoughts. Pip has never enjoyed her company, yet he dreams of their happiness together. From this, the reader can infer that Pip is unrealistic about romantic relationships.

Analogy

An analogy is a comparison of two things. The words in the analogy are connected by a certain, often undetermined relationship. Look at this analogy: moo is to cow as quack is to duck. This analogy compares the sound that a cow makes with the sound that a duck makes. Even if the word 'quack' was not given, one could figure out it is the correct word to complete the analogy based on the relationship between the words 'moo' and 'cow'. Some common relationships for analogies include synonyms, antonyms, part to whole, definition, and actor to action.

<u>Examples</u>
Determine the relationship between the words in the following analogy, then, provide a word to fill in the blank:

Doctor: heals

Mechanic: _____

Some common relationships used in analogies are synonyms, antonyms, part to whole, definition, and actor to action. In this case, the relationship between the words 'doctor' and 'heals' is actor to action. The action the doctor takes is to heal. Using this relationship, one can determine a proper word to fill in the blank. A mechanic is a person who fixes or repairs cars, thus the action that the mechanic takes is to fix or repair things. This being the case, a correct word to fill in the blank would be 'fixes' or 'repairs'.

Determine the relationship between the words in the following analogy, then, provide a word to fill in the blank:

Banana: peel

_____: leg

Some common relationships used in analogies are synonyms, antonyms, part to whole, definition, and actor to action. In this case, the relationship between the words 'peel' and 'banana' is part to whole. A banana is a whole piece of fruit and a peel is the outer part of a banana. Using this relationship as a guide, one can determine the correct word to fill in the blank, one that is the whole that a leg is part of. A leg is a part of the body, thus, a correct word to fill in the blank would be <u>body</u>.

Media

Media are methods of storing or delivering information. Mass media is a type of media, such as television, radio, or the internet, that conveys information to the general public, or the masses. Print media is a type of media that includes any printed documents, such as this study material, used to transmit information. News media is a type of mass media that includes newspapers, newsletters, television news shows, and other means of transmitting news. Another widely used type is advertising media. This includes television and radio commercials, billboards, and newspaper ads. In many cases, media are used not only to convey information, but also to affect opinion and action. For instance in advertising, the advertiser conveys biased opinions about a product, hoping to profit from the recipient of the information buying the advertised product. News media should be unbiased, but opinions can be very easily intermixed with fact, such that an undiscerning recipient may not be able to distinguish between the fact and opinion, and simply accept both as fact.

Textual evidence

Using textual evidence means referring to specific things mentioned within the text when talking about it. When one discusses a text, they want to use textual evidence to make their argument or statement stronger. Using textual evidence helps support the argument being made and gives what is being said more weight. By quoting from the text or mentioning specific details the author used, one can better support the argument they are making. An argument will be weak and unconvincing if one does not provide support; including facts, details, and evidence from texts read.

Paraphrasing and summarizing

Paraphrasing and summarizing are two methods one can use to help them understand what they read. When paraphrasing, one puts what they have read into their own words, rephrasing what the author has written to make it their own, to "translate" all of what the author says to their own words, including as many details as they can. When summarizing, on the other hand, one does not include many details, but rather simply the main idea of the text. Often times, a summary can be done in just one sentence, boiling down the author's words into just main idea.

<u>Example summary</u>
Read the following paragraph and then give a one sentence summary statement:

People used to know their bankers. Now, many people do their banking online. With a login and password, customers can have access to their accounts with up to the minute information. Users can keep track of their spending, transfer money between accounts, and pay bills online, all from the comfort of home.

In order to summarize, one has to identify the main idea and any supporting ideas in the author's work. The summary is an overview of the author's paragraph and will tell what it is about without getting into any of the details. The summary needs to be broad enough to cover all of the information in the author's paragraph. Here is a possible summary statement for the above paragraph:

> Most people nowadays find it convenient to do their banking online instead of at a branch office.

<u>Example paraphrasing</u>
Read the following sentences and then paraphrase the material:

The government is debating a new health care system for our country. The Senate and the House of Representatives have both passed bills; now they need to resolve these two bills into one bill that a majority can agree on.

When paraphrasing information, one needs to read carefully and pay attention to details, then put the material away and write or tell it in their own words. One does not want to look at the material while paraphrasing to avoid plagiarizing by accident. Here is one example of a way to paraphrase the sentences:

> Our government is trying to adopt a new health care system. The Senate has passed a bill and so has the House of Representatives. Their bills are different so now they have to compromise on one bill that can be passed.

Fact and opinion

A fact is something that is said about a subject that can be tested and proved to be true. Examples of facts include details and statistics. For example, a fact could be:

> That balloon is red.

> 85% of the kids in the class do not get enough sleep.

As both of these can be proven true, they are identified as facts.

An opinion, on the other hand, is what someone thinks about a subject. An opinion cannot be tested or proven to be true because it is subjective. One person may think one thing and another person something the complete opposite. Examples of opinions include thoughts, beliefs, and ideas. For instance, an opinion could be:

> The colors used to paint the house make it look welcoming and inviting.

> I believe that the school leadership team is acting effectively.

Authors use certain phrases to state opinions and it is important for a reader to be able to identify the author's opinion about a subject. The reader can use these phrases to help identify as an opinion, as opposed to a fact. Some phrases that indicate an opinion statement include: 'I believe,' 'I think,' 'in my opinion,' 'it seems to me,' 'it's obvious that,' 'it's clear that,' and 'they should.'

It is important that a reader be able to distinguish between a fact and an opinion. A fact is something said about a subject that can be tested and proved to be true. Examples of facts include details and statistics. An opinion is what someone thinks about a subject and cannot be tested or proven to be true, as it is subjective. One person may think one thing and another person the exact opposite. Examples of opinions include thoughts, beliefs, and ideas. The reader needs to be able to identify if something is true or merely the author's opinion in order to determine whether or not to trust the source. When something is presented factually, the reader can trust the source to be accurate and unbiased. When information presented is the author's opinion, the reader can decide for him- or herself whether or not to agree with the author.

Organizational methods to structure text

Authors organize their writing based on the purpose of their text. Some common organizational methods that authors use include: cause and effect, compare/contrast, inductive presentation of ideas, deductive presentation of ideas, and chronological order. Cause and effect is used to present the reason why something happened. Compare/contrast is used to discuss the similarities and differences between two things. Inductive presentation of ideas starts with specific examples and moves to a general conclusion. Deductive presentation of ideas starts with a general conclusion, then explains the examples used to arrive at the conclusion. Chronological order presents information in the order that it occurred.

Cause and effect and chronological order
Authors have to organize information logically so the reader can follow it and locate information within the text. Two common organizational structures are *cause and effect* and *chronological order*. In *cause and effect*, an author presents one thing that makes something else happen. For example, if one were to go to bed very late, they would be tired. The cause is going to bed late, with the effect of being tired the next

day. When using *chronological order*, the author presents information in the order that it happened. For example, biographies are written in chronological order; the subject's birth and childhood are presented first, followed by their adult life, and lastly by the events leading up to the person's death.

Example
Read the following thesis statement and discuss the organizational pattern the author will use:

While many people are content with the DVD players they already have at home, Blu-ray technology provides for better viewing of high definition video.

From this thesis statement the reader can assume that the author is going to use a deductive presentation of ideas. The author starts with the conclusion that Blu-ray technology is a better method for watching high definition video than DVD. The reader can assume that in the rest of the text, the author will discuss the reasons why he arrived at this conclusion, most likely providing details and examples that will support his conclusion. When the conclusion is presented first, then followed by specific examples, the ideas are presented in deductive order.

Example
Read the following thesis statement and discuss the organizational pattern that the author will use:

Among people who are current on the latest technologies, there is a debate over whether DVD or Blu-ray Disc is a better choice for watching and recording video.

From the thesis statement the reader can assume that the author is going to use a compare/ contrast organizational structure. The author mentions two options for watching and recording video: DVD and Blu-ray Disc. During the rest of the essay, the author will most likely describe the two technologies, giving specific examples of how they are similar and the differences that set them apart. The compare/ contrast structure is best used to discuss they similarities and differences of two things.

Example
Read the following thesis statement and discuss the organizational pattern that the author will use:

Throughout his life, Thomas Edison used his questioning and creative mind to become one of America's greatest inventors.

Based on the thesis statement, the reader can assume that the author is going to use chronological order to organize the information in the rest of the essay. The words "throughout his life" clue the reader in to the chronological organizational structure, which presents information in the order than it occurred. The author will probably discuss Edison's childhood and initial inventions first and then move on to his later queries and inventions. Chronological order is often used as the organizational structure in biographies as a way to logically present the important events in a person's life.

Outline

Example
Write a brief outline for a paragraph on large cats that will include information on the habitat and food for lions, tigers, cheetahs, and leopards:

In the paragraph described, one can break the topic into four brief sections, one for each animal. The subsections for each can be their habitat and food. Here is an example outline:

I. Large Cats
    a. Lions
        i. Habitat
        ii. Food
    b. Tigers
        i. Habitat
        ii. Food
    c. Cheetahs
        i. Habitat
        ii. Food
    d. Leopards
        i. Habitat
        ii. Food

Elements in a written response to literature

A written response to literature is one's response or reaction to a certain piece of text. When one responds to text, they should include their background knowledge on the topic, connections they can make to their own life, connections they can make to other texts they have read, and what the text makes them feel and think about. One may also include ways that they agree or disagree with the author and questions they may have for the author. Using specific evidence (i.e., quotes) from the text can support and strengthen a response.

Practice Test #1

Practice Questions

Questions 1 -12 pertain to the following passages:

Call of the Wild by Jack London

(1) Buck did not read the newspapers, or he would have known that trouble was brewing, not alone for himself, but for every tide-water dog, strong of muscle and with warm, long hair, from Puget Sound to San Diego. Because men, groping in the Arctic darkness, had found a yellow metal, and because steamship and transportation companies were booming the find, thousands of men were rushing into the Northland. These men wanted dogs, and the dogs they wanted were heavy dogs, with strong muscles by which to toil, and furry coats to protect them from the frost.

(2) Buck lived at a big house in the sun-kissed Santa Clara Valley. Judge Miller's place, it was called. It stood back from the road, half hidden among the trees, through which glimpses could be caught of the wide cool veranda that ran around its four sides. The house was approached by gravelled driveways which wound about through wide-spreading lawns and under the interlacing boughs of tall poplars. At the rear things were on even a more spacious scale than at the front. There were great stables, where a dozen grooms and boys held forth, rows of vine-clad servants' cottages, an endless and orderly array of outhouses, long grape arbors, green pastures, orchards, and berry patches. Then there was the pumping plant for the artesian well, and the big cement tank where Judge Miller's boys took their morning plunge and kept cool in the hot afternoon.

(3) And over this great demesne Buck ruled. Here he was born, and here he had lived the four years of his life. It was true, there were other dogs, There could not but be other dogs on so vast a place, but they did not count. They came and went, resided in the populous kennels, or lived obscurely in the recesses of the house after the fashion of Toots, the Japanese pug, or Ysabel, the Mexican hairless,— strange creatures that rarely put nose out of doors or set foot to ground. On the other hand, there were the fox terriers, a score of them at least, who yelped fearful promises at Toots and Ysabel looking out of the windows at them and protected by a legion of housemaids armed with brooms and mops.

(4) But Buck was neither house-dog nor kennel-dog. The whole realm was his. He plunged into the swimming tank or went hunting with the Judge's sons; he escorted Mollie and Alice, the Judge's daughters, on long twilight or early morning rambles; on wintry nights he lay at the Judge's feet before the roaring library fire; he carried the Judge's grandsons on his back, or rolled them in the grass, and guarded their footsteps through wild adventures down to the fountain in the stable yard, and even beyond, where the paddocks were, and the berry patches. Among the terriers he stalked imperiously, and Toots and Ysabel he utterly ignored, for he was king,—king over all creeping, crawling, flying things of Judge Miller's place, humans included.

(5) His father, Elmo, a huge St. Bernard, had been the Judge's inseparable companion, and Buck bid fair to follow in the way of his father. He was not so large,—he weighed only one hundred and forty pounds,—for his mother, Shep, had been a Scotch shepherd dog. Nevertheless, one hundred and forty pounds, to which was added the dignity that comes of good living and universal respect, enabled him to carry himself in right royal fashion. During the four years since his puppyhood he had lived the life of a sated aristocrat; he had a fine pride in himself, was even a trifle egotistical, as country gentlemen sometimes become because of their insular situation. But he had saved himself by not becoming a mere pampered house-dog. Hunting and kindred outdoor delights had kept down the fat and hardened his muscles; and to him, as to the cold-tubbing races, the love of water had been a tonic and a health preserver.

(6) And this was the manner of dog Buck was in the fall of 1897, when the Klondike strike dragged men from all the world into the frozen North. But Buck did not read the newspapers, and he did not know that Manuel, one of the gardener's helpers, was an undesirable acquaintance. Manuel had one besetting sin. He loved to play Chinese lottery. Also, in his gambling, he had one besetting weakness—faith in a system; and this made his damnation certain. For to play a system requires money, while the wages of a gardener's helper do not lap over the needs of a wife and numerous progeny.

(7) The Judge was at a meeting of the Raisin Growers' Association, and the boys were busy organizing an athletic club, on the memorable night of Manuel's treachery. No one saw him and Buck go off through the orchard on what Buck imagined was merely a stroll. And with the exception of a solitary man, no one saw them arrive at the little flag station known as College Park. This man talked with Manuel, and money chinked between them.

(8) "You might wrap up the goods before you deliver 'm," the stranger said gruffly, and Manuel doubled a piece of stout rope around Buck's neck under the collar.

1. What is the purpose of paragraphs 2-5?
    a. To introduce all of the story's characters
    b. To show Buck's personality
    c. To introduce Buck
    d. To show Buck's affection for Toots and Ysabel

2. Which sentence or phrase shows Buck's attitude about Judge Miller's place?
    a. They came and went, resided in the populous kennels, or lived obscurely in the recesses of the house
    b. The whole realm was his
    c. He had a fine pride in himself
    d. And to him, as to the cold-tubbing races, the love of water had been a tonic and a health preserver

3. The author uses the detail in paragraph 1 to
    a. Describe Buck's life
    b. Foreshadow Buck's story
    c. Describe the story's setting
    d. Introduce the story's villain

4. What is the significance of the Klondike strike in 1897?
    a. It will lead to changes in Buck's life
    b. It will cause more dogs to move to Judge Miller's place
    c. It changed Elmo's life
    d. It caused the Raisin Growers' Association to meet more frequently

5. The use of the word *imperiously* in paragraph four helps the reader know that Buck feels
    a. Scared
    b. Angry
    c. Happy
    d. Regal

6. The author organizes this selection mainly by
    a. Describing Buck's life in the order in which it happened
    b. Outlining Buck's history
    c. Showing Buck's life and then showing a moment of change
    d. Comparing Buck's life at Judge Miller's place to what came afterwards

7. Which answer choice best describes the purpose of the selection?
   a. To set up a story by providing background information
   b. To show Buck in a moment of heroism
   c. To give details about the Klondike strike
   d. To introduce all the dogs that live at Judge Miller's

8. In the future, Buck will probably
   a. Continue to act like the king of Judge Miller's place
   b. Reunite with his father, Elmo, and his mother, Shep
   c. Leave Judge Miller's place against his will
   d. Spend more time in the garden

9. This selection is part of a longer work. Based on the selection, what might be a theme of the larger work?
   a. Change
   b. Family
   c. Hard work
   d. Relationships

10. Paragraph 2 is mostly about:
    a. The Santa Clara Valley
    b. Judge Miller's place
    c. Buck's lifestyle
    d. The Klondike strike

11. Which sentence from the passage foreshadows the rest of the story?
    a. And over this great demesne Buck ruled
    b. These men wanted dogs, and the dogs they wanted were heavy dogs, with strong muscles by which to toil, and furry coats to protect them from the frost
    c. His father, Elmo, a huge St. Bernard, had been the Judge's inseparable companion and Buck bid fair to follow in the way of his father
    d. But he had saved himself by not becoming a mere pampered house-dog

12. What's the most logical explanation why Buck doesn't read the newspapers?
    a. He's not interested in current events
    b. He's busy exploring Judge Miller's place
    c. The Raisin Growers' Association takes all his time
    d. He's a dog

Questions 13 – 16 pertain to the following passage:

Andy Grant's Pluck by Horatio Alger

(1) The house and everything about it seemed just as it did when he left at the beginning of the school term. But Andy looked at them with different eyes.

- 20 -

(2) Then he had been in good spirits, eager to return to his school work.

Now something had happened, he did not yet know what.

(3) Mrs. Grant was in the back part of the house, and Andy was in the sitting room before she was fully aware of his presence. Then she came in from the kitchen, where she was preparing supper.

(4) Her face seemed careworn, but there was a smile upon it as she greeted her son.

(5) "Then you got my telegram?" she said. "I didn't think you would be here so soon."

(6) "I started at once, mother, for I felt anxious. What has happened? Are you all well?"

(7) "Yes, thank God, we are in fair health, but we have met with misfortune."

(8) "What is it?"

(9) "Nathan Lawrence, cashier of the bank in Benton, has disappeared with twenty thousand dollars of the bank's money."

(10) "What has that to do with father? He hasn't much money in that bank."

(11) "Your father is on Mr. Lawrence's bond to the amount of six thousand dollars."

(12) "I see," answered Andy, gravely, "How much will he lose?"

(13) "The whole of it."

(14) This, then, was what had happened. To a man in moderate circumstances, it must needs be a heavy blow.

(15) "I suppose it will make a great difference?" said Andy, inquiringly.

(16) "You can judge. Your father's property consists of this farm and three thousand dollars in government bonds. It will be necessary to sacrifice the bonds and place a mortgage of three thousand dollars on the farm."

(17) "How much is the farm worth?"

(18) "Not over six thousand dollars."

(19) "Then father's property is nearly all swept away."

(20) "Yes," said his mother, sadly. "Hereafter he will receive no help from outside interest, and will, besides, have to pay interest on a mortgage of three thousand dollars, at six per cent."

(21) "One hundred and eighty dollars."

(22) "Yes."

(23) "Altogether, then, it will diminish our income by rather more than three hundred dollars."

(24) "Yes, Andy."

(25) "That is about what my education has been costing father," said Andy, in a low voice.

(26) He began to see how this misfortune was going to affect him.

(27) "I am afraid," faltered Mrs. Grant, "that you will have to leave school."

(28) "Of course I must," said Andy, speaking with a cheerfulness which he did not feel. "And in place of going to college I must see how I can help father bear this burden."

(29) "It will be very hard upon you, Andy," said his mother, in a tone of sympathy.

(30) "I shall be sorry, of course, mother; but there are plenty of boys who don't go to college. I shall be no worse off than they."

(31) "I am glad you bear the disappointment so well, Andy. It is of you your father and I have thought chiefly since the blow fell upon us."

(32) "Who will advance father the money on mortgage, mother?"

(33) "Squire Carter has expressed a willingness to do so. He will be here this evening to talk it over."

(34) "I am sorry for that, mother. He is a hard man. If there is a chance to take advantage of father, he won't hesitate to do it."

13. As it used in paragraph 1, the phrase *different eyes* means which of the following?
    a. Andy's eyes have changed color
    b. Andy now wears glasses
    c. Andy sees that the mood in the house has changed
    d. Andy is happy to be home

14. Read this sentence from paragraph 14:

    To a man in moderate circumstances, it must needs be a heavy blow.
    The author uses the metaphor *a heavy blow* to indicate which of the following?

    a. Andy's father is in a difficult situation
    b. Andy won't be able to go back to school
    c. Andy's father has lost over six thousand dollars
    d. Andy is disappointed about his family's problems

15. Which of these is the best summary of the selection?
   a. Andy Grant comes home from school and discovers that his father has won six thousand dollars. He will use the money to buy equipment for the farm. Andy finds out that he will need to leave school in order to help his father on the farm and work for Squire Carter
   b. Andy Grant goes home and discovers that his family has fallen upon misfortune. Nathan Lawrence, the bank's cashier, has stolen twenty thousand dollars of Andy's father's money. Now that Andy's family has lost so much money, they won't be able to pay for his education and he'll have to leave school
   c. Andy Grant's father has lost six thousand dollars because Nathan Lawrence stole it. This loss will cost Andy's family a lot of money. Since Andy's family pays $300 a month for his school, he will have to stop going to school. Andy is very cheerful that he doesn't have to go to school. He decides to work for Squire Carter in order to help his family
   d. Andy Grant's family has suffered a misfortune because the bank's cashier stole money, some of which belonged to Andy's father. Without the money, Andy's family will have trouble paying its bills, including Andy's school bills. Andy will have to stop going to school. Furthermore, his father will have to borrow money

16. What phrase or sentence from the selection best shows Andy's feelings about having to leave school?
   a. He began to see how this misfortune was going to affect him
   b. Speaking with a cheerfulness which he did not feel
   c. And in place of going to college I must see how I can help father bear this burden
   d. I am sorry for that, mother

Questions 17 – 21 pertain to the following passage:

The Telegraph Boy by Horatio Alger

(1) Our hero found himself in a dirty apartment, provided with a bar, over which was a placard, inscribed:—
(2) "FREE LUNCH."
(3) "How much money have you got, Frank?" inquired Montagu Percy.
(4) "Twenty-five cents."
(5) "Lunch at this establishment is free," said Montagu; "but you are expected to order some drink. What will you have?"
(6) "I don't care for any drink except a glass of water."
(7) "All right; I will order for you, as the rules of the establishment require it; but I will drink your glass myself. Eat whatever you like."
(8) Frank took a sandwich from a plate on the counter and ate it with relish, for he was hungry. Meanwhile his companion emptied the two glasses, and ordered another.

- 23 -

(9) "Can you pay for these drinks?" asked the bar-tender, suspiciously.

(10) "Sir, I never order what I cannot pay for."

(11) "I don't know about that. You've been in here and taken lunch more than once without drinking anything."

(12) "It may be so. I will make up for it now. Another glass, please."

(13) "First pay for what you have already drunk."

(14) "Frank, hand me your money," said Montagu.

(15) Frank incautiously handed him his small stock of money, which he saw instantly transferred to the bar-tender.

(16) "That is right, I believe," said Montagu Percy.

(17) The bar-keeper nodded, and Percy, transferring his attention to the free lunch, stowed away a large amount.

(18) Frank observed with some uneasiness the transfer of his entire cash capital to the bar-tender; but concluded that Mr. Percy would refund a part after they went out. As they reached the street he broached the subject.

(19) "I didn't agree to pay for both dinners," he said, uneasily.

(20) "Of course not. It will be my treat next time. That will be fair, won't it?"

(21) "But I would rather you would give me back a part of my money. I may not see you again."

(22) "I will be in the Park to-morrow at one o'clock."

(23) "Give me back ten cents, then," said Frank, uneasily. "That was all the money I had."

(24) "I am really sorry, but I haven't a penny about me. I'll make it right to-morrow. Good-day, my young friend. Be virtuous and you will be happy."

(25) Frank looked after the shabby figure ruefully. He felt that he had been taken in and done for. His small capital had vanished, and he was adrift in the streets of a strange city without a penny.

17. Why did Frank give Mr. Percy all his money?
   a. He was feeling generous
   b. Mr. Percy offered to pay for the sandwiches
   c. He owed it to Mr. Percy
   d. He thought Mr. Percy would give him some of it back

18. What does the phrase "his small capital" mean in paragraph 25?
   a. Frank's penny
   b. Frank's twenty-five cents
   c. Frank's virtuous nature
   d. Frank's friendship with Mr. Percy

19. Why did Frank agree to eat lunch?
    a. Mr. Percy was paying for it
    b. Lunch was completely free
    c. He only needed to buy a drink
    d. He wanted to spend time with Mr. Percy

20. Is Mr. Percy likely to pay Frank back?
    a. Yes, because he never orders what he cannot pay for
    b. Yes, because he will be in the Park the next day at one o'clock
    c. No, because Frank is not virtuous or happy
    d. No, because he's shown that he does not have any money

21. What adjective best describes Frank's feelings in paragraph 25?
    a. Disappointed
    b. Incautious
    c. Uneasy
    d. Suspicious

Questions 22 – 25 pertain to both "Andy Grant's Pluck" and "The Telegraph Boy passages":

22. How are Andy and Frank similar?
    a. They both have loving families
    b. They both have experienced misfortune
    c. They both were tricked
    d. They both need money for food

23. How are "Andy Grant's Pluck" and "The Telegraph Boy" different?
    a. "Andy Grant's Pluck" explains the circumstances that led to Andy's family misfortune, and "The Telegraph Boy" does not explain how Frank ended up with no money at all
    b. Andy is all alone, but Frank has many friends who can help him
    c. In "Andy Grant's Pluck," Andy is the victim of his family's bad luck but Frank in "The Telegraph Boy" is in trouble because he lost his own money
    d. "Andy Grant's Pluck" is about how Andy was tricked, and "The Telegraph Boy" is about how Frank lost his money

24. Both selections end with the main characters
    a. Feeling hopeful about the future
    b. Looking forward to going back to school
    c. In a dangerous situation
    d. Feeling uncertain about the future

25. Which of these sentences or phrases from "Andy Grant's Pluck" could also describe how Frank in the "The Telegraph Boy" feels at the end of the selection?
a. He will receive no help from outside interest
b. I must see how I can help father bear this burden
c. Speaking with a cheerfulness which he did not feel
d. We have met with misfortune

Questions 26 -31 pertain to the following passage:

The Great Round World and What is Going On In It
By
William Beverley Harison

(1) There is a new cause for supposing that the Treaty with Great Britain will either be defeated in the Senate, or else delayed for some time to come.

(2) This new trouble concerns the building of the Nicaragua Canal.

(3) It seems a remote cause, does it not? but it only shows how closely the affairs of one nation are bound up with those of all the others. No matter what our speech, our climate, or our color, we are all a portion of the great human family, and the good of one is the good of all.

(4) The Nicaragua Canal is a water-way that will cross the narrow neck of land that makes Central America. It will connect the Atlantic Ocean with the Pacific Ocean.

(5) With the help of such a canal, ships in going to the western coast of North or South America will not need to make the long and dangerous voyage around Cape Horn.

(6) Cape Horn, you will see if you look on your map, is the extreme southerly point of South America.

(7) There are so many storms and fogs there, that the Horn, as it is called, is much dreaded by sailors.

(8) Since the invention of steam, all the steamships go through the Straits of Magellan, and save the passage round the Horn; but there is not enough wind for sailing vessels in the rocky and narrow straits, so they still have to take the outside passage.

(9) The Straits of Magellan divide the main continent of South America from a group of islands, called Tierra del Fuego, and Cape Horn is the most southerly point of this archipelago.

(10) The journey down the coast of South America on the east, and up again on the west, takes such a long time, that the desire for a canal across the narrow neck of land which joins North and South America has been in men's minds for many years.

(11) A railway was built across the Isthmus of Panama to shorten the distance, and save taking the passage round the Horn. Travellers left their ship at one side of the Isthmus, and took the train over to the

- 26 -

other, where they went on board another ship, which would take them the rest of their journey.

(12) This plan greatly increased the expense of the journey, and the canal was still so much wanted, that at last the Panama Canal was begun.

(13) You have all heard about the Panama Canal, which was to do the same work that the Nicaragua Canal is to do, that is, to connect the Atlantic and Pacific Oceans. You have probably heard how much time, labor, and human life was wasted over it, and how much trouble its failure caused in France.

(14) This Canal was to cut across the Isthmus at its very narrowest point. It was worked on for years, every one believing that it would be opened to ships before very long. Many of the maps and geographies that were printed in the eighties said that the Panama Canal would be opened in 1888, or at latest in 1889.

(15) No one expected what afterward happened. In 1889 the works were stopped for want of money; the affairs of the Canal were looked into; it was found that there had been dishonesty and fraud, and in 1892 the great Count Ferdinand de Lesseps, who built the Suez Canal, and a number of other prominent Frenchmen, were arrested for dealing dishonestly with the money subscribed for the Canal.

(16) There was a dreadful scandal; many of the high French officials had to give up their positions, and run away for fear of arrest.

(17) When the whole matter was understood, it was found that, for months before the work was stopped, the men who had charge of the Canal had decided that the work would cost such an enormous sum of money that it would be almost an impossibility to complete it.

(18) They did not have the honesty to let this be known, but allowed people to go on subscribing money, a part of which they put in their own pockets, and spent the rest in bribing the French newspapers not to tell the truth about the Canal.

(19) The worst of it was, that the money which had been subscribed was not from rich people, who would feel its loss very little, but from poor people, who put their savings, and the money they were storing away for their old age, into the Canal; and when they lost it, it meant misery and poverty to them.

(20) So the Panama Canal failed.

(21) But the project of making a canal was not given up. Two years before the idea of digging at Panama had been thought of, the ground where the Nicaragua Canal is being built had been surveyed, and thought better suited to the purpose than Panama.

(22) The reason for this was, that at Panama a long and deep cut had to be made through the mountains. This had to be done by blasting, in much the same way that the rocks are cleared away to build houses. This is a long and tedious work.

(23) The Nicaragua Canal will be 159 miles long, while the Panama, if it is ever completed, will be only 59 miles; but of these 159 miles, 117 are through the Nicaragua Lake and the San Juan River—water-ways already made by nature. For the remaining distance, there are other river-beds that will be used, and only 21 miles will actually have to be cut through.

(24) The main objection to this route for the Canal is, that there is a volcano on an island in the Nicaragua Lake, and there are always fears of eruptions and earthquakes in the neighborhood of volcanoes. A great eruption of the volcano might change the course of a river, or alter the face of the country so much, that the Canal might have to be largely remade.

26. The author mentions the treaty with Great Britain in paragraph 1 because people are concerned about
   a. A canal through Cape Horn
   b. The new Panama Canal
   c. The building of the Nicaragua Canal
   d. The Central America Canal

27. What are paragraphs 15-19 mostly about?
   a. The building of the Suez Canal
   b. The financial problems that ended the Panama Canal project
   c. The French newspapers, which did not tell the truth about the canal
   d. Ferdinand de Lesseps' experience in jail

28. Which sentence best shows the purpose for building the Nicaragua Canal?
   a. The new trouble concerns the building of the Nicaragua Canal
   b. Cape Horn, you will see if you look on your map, is the extreme southerly point of South America
   c. There are so many storms and fogs there, that the Horn, as it is called, is much dreaded by sailors
   d. Since the invention of steam, all the steamships go through the Straits of Magellan

29. What is the tone of this passage?
   a Informational
   b. Humorous
   c. Mysterious
   d. Angry

30. Why will the Nicaragua Canal be easier to build than the Panama Canal?
   a. It is 100 miles longer than the Panama Canal
   b. It needs to be blasted through the mountains
   c. The San Juan River is already a complete canal
   d. Most of the canal will go through existing waterways

31. Look at the time line below.

Canals Around the World

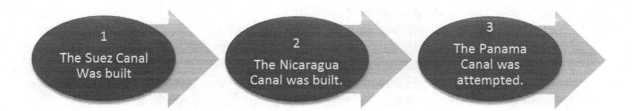

According to the passage, what is the correct order of the time line?
    a. No change
    b. 1, 3, 2
    c. 2, 1, 3
    d. 3, 1, 2

32. The author probably wrote this selection to
    a. Argue against the building of the Nicaragua Canal
    b. Argue for the building of the Nicaragua Canal
    c. Explain the problems that ended the Panama Canal project
    d. Discuss new plans for a canal

33. Which words in paragraph 22 help the reader know what *blasting* means?
    a. Long and deep cut
    b. Had to be made
    c. To build houses
    d. Long and tedious work

34. What is the main problem in building the Nicaragua Canal?
    a. Many of the financial backers, like Ferdinand de Lesseps, are in jail
    b. The route needs to be cut through mountains
    c. The Nicaragua Canal is interrupting the treaty with Great Britain
    d. The canal route goes past a volcano

35. Why does the author discuss the Panama Canal?
    a. He is highlighting the other great canal in Central America
    b. He is explaining the reasons why a canal is needed
    c. He is showing the first canal that was attempted and why it failed
    d. He is explaining how sailors avoid going around Cape Horn

36. Read this phrase from paragraph 19: *And when they lost it, it meant misery and poverty to them.* The author uses this sentence to show:
  a. The people who suffered the most from the failure to build the Panama Canal
  b. Why the Panama Canal failed
  c. Rich people suffered the most from the failure to build the Panama Canal
  d. The project of making a canal was not given up

37. The Nicaragua Canal will?
  a. Make sailing longer and more dangerous
  b. Help ships avoid Cape Horn
  c. Cause more people to take the train across the Isthmus of Panama
  d. Cut across the Isthmus at its very narrowest point

Questions 38 – 48 pertain to the following passages:

"The Ettrick Shepherd" by James Baldwin

Part I

(1) In Scotland there once lived a poor shepherd whose name was James Hogg. His father and grandfather and great-grandfather had all been shepherds.

(2) It was his business to take care of the sheep which belonged to a rich landholder by the Ettrick Water. Sometimes he had several hundreds of lambs to look after. He drove these to the pastures on the hills and watched them day after day while they fed on the short green grass.

(3) He had a dog which he called Sirrah. This dog helped him watch the sheep. He would drive them from place to place as his master wished. Sometimes he would take care of the whole flock while the shepherd was resting or eating his dinner.

(4) One dark night James Hogg was on the hilltop with a flock of seven hundred lambs. Sirrah was with him. Suddenly a storm came up. There was thunder and lightning; the wind blew hard; the rain poured.

(5) The poor lambs were frightened. The shepherd and his dog could not keep them together. Some of them ran towards the east, some towards the west, and some towards the south.

(6) The shepherd soon lost sight of them in the darkness. With his lighted lantern in his hand, he went up and down the rough hills calling for his lambs.

(7) Two or three other shepherds joined him in the search. All night long they sought for the lambs.

(8) Morning came and still they sought. They looked, as they thought, in every place where the lambs might have taken shelter.

(9) At last James Hogg said, "It's of no use; all we can do is to go home and tell the master that we have lost his whole flock."

(10) They had walked a mile or two towards home, when they came to the edge of a narrow and deep ravine. They looked down, and at the bottom they saw some lambs huddled together among the rocks. And there was Sirrah standing guard over them and looking all around for help. "These must be the lambs that rushed off towards the south," said James Hogg.

(11) The men hurried down and soon saw that the flock was a large one.

(12) "I really believe they are all here," said one.

(13) They counted them and were surprised to find that not one lamb of the great flock of seven hundred was missing.

(14) How had Sirrah managed to get the three scattered divisions together? How had he managed to drive all the frightened little animals into this place of safety?

(15) Nobody could answer these questions. But there was no shepherd in
Scotland that could have done better than Sirrah did that night.

(16) Long afterward James Hogg said, "I never felt so grateful to any creature below the sun as I did to Sirrah that morning."

Part II

(17) When James Hogg was a boy, his parents were too poor to send him to school. By some means, however, he learned to read; and after that he loved nothing so much as a good book.

(18) There were no libraries near him, and it was hard for him to get books. But he was anxious to learn. Whenever he could buy or borrow a volume of prose or verse he carried it with him until he had read it through. While watching his flocks, he spent much of his time in reading. He loved poetry and soon began to write poems of his own. These poems were read and admired by many people.

(19) The name of James Hogg became known all over Scotland. He was often called the Ettrick Shepherd, because he was the keeper of sheep near the Ettrick Water.

(20) Many of his poems are still read and loved by children as well as by grown up men and women. Here is one:

A Boy's Song

Where the pools are bright and deep,
Where the gray trout lies asleep,
Up the river and o'er the lea,
That's the way for Billy and me.
Where the blackbird sings the latest,

Where the hawthorn blooms the sweetest,
Where the nestlings chirp and flee,
That's the way for Billy and me.
Where the mowers mow the cleanest,
Where the hay lies thick and greenest,
There to trace the homeward bee,
That's the way for Billy and me.
Where the hazel bank is steepest,
Where the shadow falls the deepest,
Where the clustering nuts fall free,
That's the way for Billy and me.
Why the boys should drive away,
Little maidens from their play,
Or love to banter and fight so well,
That's the thing I never could tell.
But this I know, I love to play
In the meadow, among the hay—
Up the water, and o'er the lea,
That's the way for Billy and me.

38. Why is James Hogg called the Ettrick Shepherd?
   a. He lived in Scotland
   b. He kept sheep
   c. He lived near Ettrick Water
   d. He lived near Ettrick Water and kept sheep

39. Which of the following best describes the problem in paragraphs 1-16?
   a. The sheep ran away and James Hogg couldn't find them
   b. A storm came up and Sirrah got scared
   c. James Hogg had trouble of taking care of such a large flock
   d. James Hogg got lost in the darkness

40. What does the phrase, *Where the blackbird sings the latest*, from the poem "A Boy's Song" refer to?
   a. James and Billy's favorite type of bird
   b. A place where James and Billy like to play
   c. The hay
   d. James and Billy's favorite song

41. In paragraphs 11-16, how does James know all the sheep were in the ravine?
   a. Sirrah told him
   b. He counted the sheep
   c. He rounded them all up from the east, the west, and the south
   d. He was the best shepherd in Scotland

42. What does the poem show about the narrator's personality?
    a. He is playful
    b. He is afraid of shadows
    c. He is not curious
    d. He does not like to explore things

43. Use the story map to answer the question below.

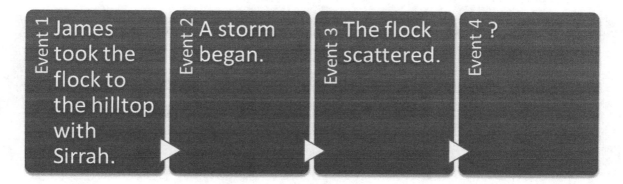

Which of these belongs in the empty box on the story map?
    a. James wrote a poem about his sheep
    b James searched for the flock
    c. James lived in Scotland
    d. Sirrah gathered up all of the sheep

44. Why did James Hogg take care of the sheep?
    a. He took care of them as a favor to the landholder
    b. He loved the lambs
    c. Taking care of the sheep was his job
    d. He liked spending time with Sirrah

45. In paragraph 18, the word *prose* means
    a. Book
    b. Writing
    c. Library
    d. To learn

46. What's the most important idea is expressed in "A Boy's Song"?
    a. Billy and the narrator are great friends
    b. Being a shepherd is hard work
    c. The narrator enjoys nature
    d. Billy and the narrator fight frequently

47. In paragraph 8, the word *sought* means?
    a. To see
    b. To think
    c. To seek
    d. to come

48. Which word best describes how James felt after he located the sheep?
    a. Surprised
    b. Scared
    c. Tired
    d. Disappointed

Answers and Explanations

1. C: The correct answer choice is C because paragraphs 2-5 introduce Buck and the setting in which he lives. The paragraphs accomplish this introduction by giving many detailed facts, such as the detail in paragraph 5 about the times he escorted Mollie and Alice on walks. Choice A is incorrect because two new characters, Manuel and the stranger, are introduced in paragraphs 7 and 8. While aspects of paragraphs 2-5 show Buck's personality, choice B is incorrect because the paragraphs also give other details about Buck, such as information about his parents and appearance. Choice D is incorrect because Toots and Ysabel are only mentioned in paragraphs 3 and 4. Furthermore, paragraph 4 says that he utterly ignored Toots and Ysabel, not that he is affectionate towards them.

2. B: The correct answer is choice B because the sentence indicates that Buck felt as if he owned or ruled over Judge Miller's place. The word *realm* indicates that the sentence is referring to everything. Choice A is incorrect because it talks about other dogs that came and went but does not show Buck's attitude towards them or Judge Miller's place. Choice C is incorrect because it shows Buck's opinion of himself but not his opinion of Judge Miller's place. Choice A is incorrect because it describes something that Buck enjoys, but does not give his attitude about the house and grounds at Judge Miller's.

3. B: The correct answer is choice B because details in the passage foreshadow what might happen to Buck. Phrases like "trouble was brewing" or "these men wanted dogs" indicate that one of the dogs men want or Buck might be heading for trouble. Choice A is incorrect because the paragraph does not give details about Buck's life; later paragraphs give those details. Choice C is incorrect because the paragraph does not give setting details. Setting details about Buck's current situation are given in later paragraphs. Choice D is incorrect because the paragraph does not describe any characters other than Buck; it does not indicate that Buck is the villain.

4. A: Choice A is the correct answer because the Klondike strike has caused people to look for dogs like Buck. Although paragraph 1 does not directly mention the Klondike strike, the reader can infer from paragraph 6 that the events discussed refer to the Klondike strike. Choice B is incorrect because paragraph 3 makes it clear that dogs came and went even before the Klondike strike. Choice C is incorrect because Elmo is Buck's father but not a main character in the story. Choice D is incorrect because the passage does not draw a connection between the Klondike strike and the frequency of the Raisin Growers' Association's meetings.

5. D: Choice D is correct because the sentence indicates that Buck considers himself to be like a king. Kings or royalty are often considered regal. Choice A is incorrect because nothing in the paragraph indicates that Buck is scared; in fact, Buck is like a king, which makes him unlikely to be scared of the other dogs. Choice B is incorrect

because Buck doesn't indicate anger, which could be shown by barking or growling. Choice C is incorrect because *regal* is referring to Buck feeling like a king, which is unrelated to his happiness.

6. C: Choice C is correct because the first part of the passage mostly describes Buck's life, but the passage ends in a moment of change when the stranger wraps a piece of rope around Buck's neck. Choice A is incorrect because the passage does not describe a sequence of events as they happen. Instead the passage gives an overview of how Buck lived before the moment of change. Although part of the passage describes Buck's history, the passage also describes the moment in which his life changes, making choice B incorrect. Choice D is incorrect because the passage only describes life at Judge Miller's place but doesn't describe what came afterwards.

7. A: The correct answer is choice A because most of the passage provides background information about Buck's life and personality. Choice B is incorrect because the passage does not describe any moments in which Buck is acting heroic; instead, it describes Buck's regular interactions with the other people and animals at Judge Miller's place. Choice C is incorrect because the passage only briefly mentions the Klondike strike. The majority of the passage describes Buck's life. Choice D is incorrect because the other dogs are described in paragraphs 3 and 4. The rest of the passage focuses on Buck.

8. C: The correct answer is choice C because the stranger ties a rope around Buck's neck. This action indicates that Buck will be forced to leave Judge Miller's place. Choice A is incorrect because the end of the passage indicates that Buck might be forced to leave Judge Miller's place, which means he won't be able to continue to act like a king. Choice B is incorrect because the passage does not mention Buck or Shep at the end; Buck's parents are only mentioned in paragraph 5 when the passage describes Buck's family background. Although Manuel is a gardener, choice D is incorrect because Buck is likely leaving the garden to go away with the stranger, which means he won't be able to spend more time in the garden.

9. A: The best answer is choice A because the passage begins by setting up Buck's life and then showing a moment where his life is about to drastically change. Choice B is incorrect because only paragraph 5 refers to family; this is not a big enough portion of the passage to imply that the larger selection is about family. Although Buck might need to work hard in the future, choice C is incorrect because the passage does not have that many clues about upcoming hard work. Choice C is incorrect because the passage does not spend time showing that Buck strongly values relationships. The end of the passage indicates that Buck is about to experience a moment of change.

10. B: The best answer is choice B because paragraph 2 describes Judge Miller's place in great detail, including a description of the house, the driveway, the stables, and the outhouses. Choice A is incorrect because the paragraph only says that his place is in the Santa Clara Valley; however, the paragraph does not describe the

valley in detail (it only describes it as sun-kissed). Choice C is incorrect because paragraphs 3 and 4 describe Buck's lifestyle, not paragraph 2. Choice D is incorrect because paragraph 2 does not mention the Klondike strike. The strike is referred to in paragraphs 1 and 6.

11. B: The correct answer is choice B because the sentence talks about how the men want dogs; the sentence foreshadows that Buck may be the type of dog that the men want. Choice A is incorrect because it refers to Buck's attitude around Judge Miller's place but does not hint at what might be coming next. Although part of the sentence indicates that Buck hopes to follow in Elmo's footsteps, the rest of the sentence simply describes Buck's father. Choice B better foreshadows what's going to happen in the story because it more closely relates to the events in paragraph 7 and 8. Choice D is incorrect because the sentence describes Buck's personality and interests without giving clues about what's going to happen next.

12. D: The best answer is choice D because, as a dog, Buck can't read. Although Buck may not be interested in current events, choice A is incorrect because choice D is a more logical answer. Choices B and C are also incorrect because the logic that Buck doesn't read the newspapers is drawn from the fact that dogs can't read.

13. C: The correct answer is C because Andy and his family were in good spirits, or happy, when he left for school at the beginning of the term. Now that he's returned, he knows something is wrong, but isn't sure what it is. Choice A is incorrect because the passage does not discuss Andy's eye color. The phrase *different eyes* is used metaphorically and does not literally mean that Andy has different eyes. For this reason, choice B is also incorrect. Choice D is incorrect because Andy is uneasy rather than happy. He knows something bad has happened.

14. A: Choice A is the correct answer because the phrase *a heavy blow* refers to the very difficult situation that Andy's father now finds himself in. The difficult situation hit him like a hammer, or heavy blow, because it was sudden and very financially painful. While it's true that Andy can't go back to school, choice B is incorrect because the sentence refers to Andy's father rather than Andy. Although losing six thousand dollars is part of the heavy blow, choice C is incorrect because the sentence does not show how much money Andy's father lost. The reader finds out the amount of money in paragraph 11, while the sentence in the question does not appear until paragraph 14. Choice D is incorrect because the sentence does not refer to Andy.

15. D: While parts of the other answer choices are correct, the best answer is choice D because it is the only choice that correctly summarizes the passage. Choice A is incorrect because Andy's father has not won six thousand dollars; he has lost that amount of money. Choice B is incorrect because Nathan Lawrence has stolen twenty thousand dollars, but only six thousand of that amount belonged to Andy's father. Choice C is incorrect because Andy is not cheerful that he doesn't have to go back to school; he likes school and is very disappointed.

16. B: The reader learns in paragraph 1 that Andy likes school. When Andy finds out he can't return to school, he is disappointed but he makes his voice sound cheerful when he's speaking to his family. Choice A is incorrect because it doesn't show Andy's feelings; it just shows that Andy knows how the family's misfortune will affect his studies. Choice C is incorrect because it simply contains Andy's new plans for the future and does not show his emotions. Choice D is incorrect even though this sentence does show Andy's emotions. However, this sentence refers to Andy's opinion about Squire Carter and not about returning to school.

17. D: Choice D is the correct answer. In paragraph 19, Frank says that he didn't agree to pay for both dinners, and then in paragraph 23 he asks for at least ten cents back. These two examples show that Frank thought Mr. Percy would return some of his money. Choice A is incorrect because Frank didn't intend to give all his money even though it may have been generous for Frank to buy Mr. Percy a drink. Choice B is incorrect because Mr. Percy didn't offer to pay for anything; in fact, he took money and didn't repay it. Choice C is incorrect because the passage does not indicate that Mr. Percy owes the money. Instead, it shows Mr. Percy tricking Frank in order to get Frank to buy him drinks.

18. B: The correct answer is choice B because the word *capital* refers to money. The reader can use the context of the passage to find the meaning of *capital*. Frank lost his twenty-five cents, which means his capital had vanished. Even though *capital* refers to money, choice A is incorrect because Frank had twenty-five cents rather than just a penny. Choice C is incorrect because Mr. Percy is the one who calls Frank virtuous. Choice D is incorrect because it's not clear if Frank had a friendship with Mr. Percy in the first place. Therefore, his friendship would not have vanished.

19. C: Frank knew he did not have much money, but when he saw that he would get a free lunch if he bought a drink, he was willing to eat it. Even though Mr. Percy handed the bartender the money, choice A is incorrect because Mr. Percy handed over Frank's money. Choice B is incorrect because lunch was not completely free; he needed to buy a drink in order to get the free sandwiches. Choice D is incorrect because nothing in the passage indicates that Frank wanted to spend time with Mr. Percy. Instead, paragraph 8 says that Frank was hungry.

20. D: Choice D is the best answer because Mr. Percy used Frank's money in order to get the drinks. Even though Mr. Percy claims that he'll pay Frank tomorrow, the reader can infer that he is probably lying. Choice C is incorrect because Mr. Percy tells Frank to be virtuous and happy as a way of dismissing Frank. However, he does not withhold the money because he feels that Frank is undeserving. Choice A is incorrect because Mr. Percy ordered drinks that he could not pay for with his own money. Although Mr. Percy says he'll be in the park, choice B is incorrect because Mr. Percy might be lying.

21. A: Choice A is the correct answer because Frank has realized that he has just lost all his money. The word *ruefully* shows that Frank is disappointed. Choice B is incorrect because Frank acted incautiously earlier in the passage when he gave Mr. Percy all his money. By paragraph 25, Frank is no longer incautious. Choice C is incorrect because Frank feels uneasy in paragraph 23. By paragraph 25, Frank realizes that Mr. Percy has cheated him. Choice D is incorrect because Frank is no longer suspicious about Mr. Percy's actions; he already knows that Mr. Percy is not going to repay him.

22. B: The best answer is choice B because both Andy and Frank experience a form of misfortune. Andy's misfortune is that his family has lost money and he can't return to school. Frank's misfortune is that he is all alone in the city and does not have any money. Choice A is incorrect because only Andy has a loving family; paragraph 25 of *The Telegraph Boy* shows that Frank is all alone. Choice C is incorrect because only Frank was tricked. Andy's family lost money because a banker stole it from his father. Choice D is incorrect because only *The Telegraph Boy* shows that Frank experiences hunger. *Andy Grant's Pluck* does not indicate that Andy will have trouble buying food.

23. C: The correct answer is choice C because Andy has no control over his family's finances, while Frank's poor decision to trust Mr. Percy led to his misfortune. Although *The Telegraph Boy* does not explain how Frank ended up alone with only twenty-five cents, choice A is incorrect because *The Telegraph Boy* does show how he ended up with no money at all. Choice B is incorrect because Andy is not all alone (he has his family); similarly, Frank does not have many friends (he is all alone). Choice D is incorrect because Andy was not tricked; instead, his father was robbed.

24. D: The correct answer is D because both selections end after the main characters have suffered misfortune. They don't know what the future holds for them. Choice A is incorrect because the characters have only experienced bad things; they are not feeling hopeful. Choice B is incorrect because Andy in *Andy Grant's Pluck* can't afford to go back to school. Furthermore, Frank in *The Telegraph Boy* never mentions school. Choice C is incorrect because the characters are not in immediate danger; they are uncertain about their future, but there are no threatening things around them.

25. C: The correct answer is choice C because the sentence shows that Andy feels disappointed, or the opposite of cheerful. Frank also feels disappointed after he loses all his money. Choice A is incorrect because the sentence simply describes Andy's father's problem; it does not show feelings. Choice B is incorrect because it shows Andy's determination to help his father; *The Telegraph Boy* does not have any moments where Frank shows determination. Choice D is incorrect because it is stating a fact rather than a feeling.

26. C: The correct answer is C because paragraph 2 says, "This new trouble concerns the building of the Nicaragua Canal." Choice A is incorrect because paragraph 5 says

that people are looking for a way to avoid going around Cape Horn; sailors would be happy for a canal. Choice B is incorrect because the Panama Canal is an older, failed project. Paragraph D is incorrect because there is no canal called the Central America Canal. There are two possible canals that, if completed, would cut across Central America: the Nicaragua Canal and the Panama Canal.

27. B: The correct answer choice is B because paragraphs 15-19 detail the many financial problems that hurt the Panama Canal project. These problems include the dishonesty of several people involved in building the canal. Even though paragraph 15 mentions the Suez Canal, choice A is incorrect because the paragraph only mentions the Suez Canal to explain who Ferdinand de Lesseps is. Paragraph 18 does mention the French newspapers, but choice C is incorrect because paragraphs 15-19 are mostly about the problems that hurt the Panama Canal. While the bribing of the newspapers was one of the problems, it wasn't the entire one. Choice D is incorrect because the paragraphs don't go into detail about Ferdinand de Lesseps' time in jail; they only mention that he went to jail.

28. C: The correct answer is C because the sentence shows the dangers of going around Cape Horn. Choice A is incorrect because the sentence only discusses the way in which the Nicaragua Canal is affecting the treaty with Great Britain. Choice B is incorrect because it only details the location of Cape Horn without explaining why this location could encourage people to build a canal. Choice D is incorrect because it discusses steamships without explaining why a canal is needed.

29. A: The correct answer is A, informational, because the author includes many factual details about the Nicaragua and Panama Canals. Choice B is incorrect because the author strictly gives facts and does not include jokes that would make the passage humorous. Choice C is incorrect because the author doesn't withhold details that would add mystery to the passive. Choice D is incorrect because the author does not show emotions such as anger; he has an objective tone.

30. D: The passage explains in paragraph 23 that the Nicaragua Canal will go through existing waterways, which means that the builders will not have to cut through much land. Choice A is incorrect because, even though the Nicaragua Canal is longer, only 21 of those miles need to be cut through. This number contrasts with the 59 miles of the Panama Canal that needed to be cut through. Choice B is incorrect because the Panama Canal needed to be cut through the mountains, not the Nicaragua Canal. Choice C is incorrect because the passage does not say that the San Juan River is a canal. It simply says in paragraph 23 that the Nicaragua Canal will go through the San Juan River.

31. B: Although the passage does not give the date of the building of the Suez Canal, it does imply in paragraph 15 that the Suez Canal was built before the Panama and Nicaragua Canals when it says "the great Count Ferdinand de Lesseps, who built the Suez Canal." The passage also indicates that the Panama Canal was attempted before the Nicaragua Canal; the reason the Nicaragua Canal needed to be built was because

the Panama Canal failed. Choices A, C, and D are incorrect because they do not show the correct chronological order.

32. D: The correct answer is D because the author is discussing the new plans for a canal, which will be the Nicaragua Canal. The author does this by giving some background of canals in Central America and describing details of the Nicaragua Canal. Choices A and B are incorrect because the author is very objective and does not argue for or against the Nicaragua Canal project; instead, he just gives information. Although the author does explain the problems that ended the Panama Canal project (in paragraph 15-20), this description is a small portion of the passage. The main purpose is to describe the issues surrounding the Nicaragua Canal.

33. A: The correct answer is A because blasting will create a long and deep cut in the in the earth. The first sentence of paragraph 22 says that a long and deep cut needed to be made. The next sentence says that this cut will be made by blasting. Choice B is incorrect because the phrase 'had to be made' doesn't give details about how blasting works. Choice C is incorrect because the phrase 'to build houses' talks about building something up rather than blasting something away. Choice D is incorrect because, while blasting may be long and tedious work, the phrase does not describe what blasting it is. It just describes the type of work that blasting is.

34. D: Choice D is the correct answer because paragraph 24 says that there is a volcano in Nicaragua Lake, which the canal will go through. Choice A is incorrect because Ferdinand de Lesseps and the other people in jail backed the Panama Canal, not the Nicaragua Canal. Choice B is incorrect because paragraph 22 shows that the Panama Canal, not the Nicaragua Canal, went through the mountains. Although paragraphs 1 and 2 say that the treaty may be defeated or delayed, this treaty is not a problem in building the canal. In contrast, the building of the canal affects the treaty.

35. C: The correct answer is C because the author wants to explain what happened in the past with the Panama Canal so readers can understand the history as well as possible problems with the Nicaragua Canal. Choice A is incorrect because the Panama Canal was never completed, which means it's not the other great canal in Central America. Choice B is incorrect because the author explains why the canal is needed in paragraphs 4-11. These paragraphs come before the discussion of the Panama Canal. Choice D is incorrect sailors still needed to go around Cape Horn because the Panama Canal was never completed. If the Nicaragua Canal is completed, the sailors will then be able to avoid Cape Horn.

36. A: The correct answer is A because the sentence discusses the people who, according to the passage, were not rich, but lost money on the Panama Canal. These people suffered the most because they fell into deeper poverty. Choice B is incorrect because the sentence shows who suffered but does not show the problems that caused the money loss. Choice C is incorrect because paragraph 19 says that people

who were not rich are the people who lost the money. Choice D is incorrect because paragraph 20 says that the canal failed and that the project was not completed.

37. B: The correct answer is choice B because the passage explains that the only way for sailing vessels to get from the Atlantic Ocean to the Pacific Ocean is to go around Cape Horn. A canal will cut across Central America so that ships no longer need to go around Cape Horn. Choice A is incorrect because the canal will do the opposite by making sailing less dangerous. Choice C is incorrect because people needed to take the train before the canal was built. The train was the only way for people to go between shores while avoiding Cape Horn. Choice D is incorrect because the Panama Canal was planned to cut across at the narrowest point. The Nicaragua Canal would be 100 miles longer.

38. D: The correct answer is D because paragraph 19 says that he lived near Ettrick Water and that he was a keeper of sheep. Choice A is incorrect because he didn't get his nickname because he was Scottish; however, people all over Scotland knew who he was and called him the Ettrick Shepherd. Choices B and C are only partially correct. Both answers contributed to his nickname. Since choice D includes both, it is the best answer.

39. A: The passage says that the sheep scattered during the storm. James couldn't find them in the dark, although he did find them the next day. Choice B is incorrect because the passage does not say that Sirrah was scared; it says that the sheep were scared. Choice C is incorrect because paragraph 2 says that James sometimes watched several hundred sheep; he only had a problem with so many sheep when they became scared by the storm. Choice D is incorrect because the passage doesn't say that James got lost; instead, paragraph 6 says that he *lost sight* of the sheep. He knew where he was, but couldn't find the sheep.

40. B: The best answer is choice B because the poem describes several of the narrator's favorite places. The key word from the phrase is 'where'. The phrase is describing a specific place. Choice A is incorrect because the poem does not indicate that the narrator and Billy prefer blackbirds to other birds. Choice C is incorrect because the phrase "Where the blackbird sings the latest" is referring to the meadow. The next verse discusses the hay. Choice D is incorrect because the narrator doesn't say that the blackbird's song is his favorite song; he just mentions the song.

41. B: Choice B is correct because paragraph 13 says that James and the other shepherds counted the sheep to determine that they were all there. Choice A is incorrect because Sirrah is a dog and cannot speak. Choice C is incorrect because Sirrah rounded up the sheep, not James. Choice D is incorrect because the passage does not say he was the best shepherd; in fact, the passage does not describe the quality of his skills at all.

42. A: The correct answer is A because the poem shows a sense of wonder and excitement. The last verse also says, "I love to play", which shows how much the narrator likes to play and have fun. Choice B is incorrect because the narrator does not show fear. Instead, he shows an enthusiasm for life. Choice C is incorrect because the poem shows a lot of curiosity; the narrator describes all his favorite places and may be curious about them. Choice D is incorrect because the narrator demonstrates his love of exploring when he describes all the details of the meadow, the hay, the water, and the lea.

43. B: The correct answer is B because paragraph 6 says that James started searching for the sheep once he realized they were gone. Choice A is incorrect because the selection does not indicate that James wrote a poem immediately after losing the sheep. Furthermore, the poem in the passage is not about the sheep. Choice C is incorrect because James always lived in Scotland; the answer choice is not an event that happened after he lost the sheep. While it's true that Sirrah gathered up the sheep, choice D is incorrect because it happened after James searched for the sheep.

44. C: The correct answer is choice C because paragraph 2 says that it was his business to take care of the sheep, which means that it was his job. Choice A is incorrect because the passage shows that being a shepherd is his business. He makes money from doing it, which means he's not doing a favor. Choice B is incorrect for the same reason; James may like the sheep, but he takes care of them to earn money. Choice D is also incorrect; while James liked Sirrah and says in paragraph 16 that he is grateful to him, James is a shepherd because it's his family's business.

45. B: The correct answer is B. The passage says that he read through the prose, which implies that the prose is a form of writing. While the prose is in a book, choice A is incorrect because the word 'volume' is referring to the book. Choice C is incorrect because the paragraph says that no libraries were near James Hogg. When he wanted a book of prose, he needed to buy or borrow it. Choice D is incorrect because he may have learned from the book, but 'prose' does not mean to learn. It is a noun that means a type of writing.

46. A: The correct answer is A because the narrator frequently mentions doing things with Billy. The phrase "That's the way for Billy and me" shows that the narrator and Billy probably spend a lot of time together and are friends. Choice B is incorrect because the poem does not refer to being a shepherd at all. While the poem expresses the narrator's loves nature, the repeated mention of Billy at the end of each verse emphasizes the close friendship between the narrator and Billy. Choice D is incorrect because the poem indicates that Billy and the narrator are friends. Although the third verse mentions fighting, it does not refer to fighting with Billy.

47. C: It is clear from paragraph 7 that James and the other shepherds are looking for the sheep. The second sentence of paragraph 8 also shows that they are looking for the sheep. Choice A is incorrect because 'sought' means to look for something, not to see something, as shown in paragraphs 7 and 8. While the word *sought* rhymes with *thought*, it means to seek or look for something, as indicated by the second sentence of the paragraph. Choice D is incorrect because James and the shepherds are looking for the sheep.

48. A: James felt surprised because Sirrah managed to gather all the sheep; the selection says he's surprised in paragraph 13. Choice B is incorrect because, while James might have been scared during the storm, he was relieved when he found the sheep. While James might have felt tired after staying up all night, choice A is a better answer than choice C because the passage says that he and the shepherds were surprised. Choice D is incorrect because James had no reason to be disappointed; he found the sheep he thought he had lost and was happy.

Practice Test #2

Practice Questions

Questions 1 – 12 pertain to the following passage:

"The Cruel Crane Outwitted" from Indian Fairy Tales

(1) Long ago the Bodisat was born to a forest life as the Genius of a tree standing near a certain lotus pond.

(2) Now at that time the water used to run short at the dry season in a certain pond, not over large, in which there were a good many fish. And a crane thought on seeing the fish.

(3) "I must outwit these fish somehow or other and make a prey of them."

(4) And he went and sat down at the edge of the water, thinking how he should do it.

(5) When the fish saw him, they asked him, "What are you sitting there for, lost in thought?"

(6) "I am sitting thinking about you," said he.

(7) "Oh, sir! what are you thinking about us?" said they.

(8) "Why," he replied; "there is very little water in this pond, and but little for you to eat; and the heat is so great! So I was thinking, 'What in the world will these fish do now?'"

(9) "Yes, indeed, sir! what *are* we to do?" said they.

(10) "If you will only do as I bid you, I will take you in my beak to a fine large pond, covered with all the kinds of lotuses, and put you into it," answered the crane.

(11) "That a crane should take thought for the fishes is a thing unheard of, sir, since the world began. It's eating us, one after the other, that you're aiming at."

(12) "Not I! So long as you trust me, I won't eat you. But if you don't believe me that there is such a pond, send one of you with me to go and see it."

(13) Then they trusted him, and handed over to him one of their number—a big fellow, blind of one eye, whom they thought sharp enough in any emergency, afloat or ashore.

(14) Him the crane took with him, let him go in the pond, showed him the whole of it, brought him back, and let him go again close to the other fish. And he told them all the glories of the pond.

(15) And when they heard what he said, they exclaimed, "All right, sir! You may take us with you."

(16) Then the crane took the old purblind fish first to the bank of the other pond, and alighted in a Varana-tree growing on the bank there.

- 45 -

But he threw it into a fork of the tree, struck it with his beak, and killed it; and then ate its flesh, and threw its bones away at the foot of the tree. Then he went back and called out:

(17) "I've thrown that fish in; let another one come."

(18) And in that manner he took all the fish, one by one, and ate them, till he came back and found no more!

(19) But there was still a crab left behind there; and the crane thought he would eat him too, and called out:

(20) "I say, good crab, I've taken all the fish away, and put them into a fine large pond. Come along. I'll take you too!"

(21) "But how will you take hold of me to carry me along?"

(22) "I'll bite hold of you with my beak."

(23) "You'll let me fall if you carry me like that. I won't go with you!"

(24) "Don't be afraid! I'll hold you quite tight all the way."

(25) Then said the crab to himself, "If this fellow once got hold of fish, he would never let them go in a pond! Now if he should really put me into the pond, it would be capital; but if he doesn't—then I'll cut his throat, and kill him!" So he said to him:

(26) "Look here, friend, you won't be able to hold me tight enough; but we crabs have a famous grip. If you let me catch hold of you round the neck with my claws, I shall be glad to go with you."

(27) And the other did not see that he was trying to outwit him, and agreed. So the crab caught hold of his neck with his claws as securely as with a pair of blacksmith's pincers, and called out, "Off with you, now!"

(28) And the crane took him and showed him the pond, and then turned off towards the Varana-tree.

(29) "Uncle!" cried the crab, "the pond lies that way, but you are taking me this way!"

(30) "Oh, that's it, is it?" answered the crane. "Your dear little uncle, your very sweet nephew, you call me! You mean me to understand, I suppose, that I am your slave, who has to lift you up and carry you about with him! Now cast your eye upon the heap of fish-bones lying at the root of yonder Varana-tree. Just as I have eaten those fish, every one of them, just so I will devour you as well!"

(31) "Ah! those fishes got eaten through their own stupidity," answered the crab; "but I'm not going to let you eat *me*. On the contrary, is it *you* that I am going to destroy. For you in your folly have not seen that I was outwitting you. If we die, we die both together; for I will cut off this head of yours, and cast it to the ground!" And so saying, he gave the crane's neck a grip with his claws, as with a vice.

(32) Then gasping, and with tears trickling from his eyes, and trembling with the fear of death, the crane beseeched him, saying, "O my Lord! Indeed I did not intend to eat you. Grant me my life!"

(33) "Well, well! step down into the pond, and put me in there."

(34) And he turned round and stepped down into the pond, and placed the crab on the mud at its edge. But the crab cut through its neck as clean as one would cut a lotus-stalk with a hunting-knife, and then only entered the water!

(35) When the Genius who lived in the Varana-tree saw this strange affair, he made the wood resound with his plaudits, uttering in a pleasant voice the verse:

(36) "The villain, though exceeding clever,
Shall prosper not by his villainy.
He may win indeed, sharp-witted in deceit,
But only as the Crane here from the Crab!"

1. In paragraph 26, why does the crab makes plans to defend himself?
   a. He's worried that he'll fall
   b. He's worried the crane won't really take him to the pond
   c. He's friends with the crane
   d. He's glad to go with the crane

2. Why are the fish skeptical of the crane?
   a. The crane likes to help out fish
   b. The crane is making the pond run dry
   c. The crane likes to eat fish
   d. They might fall out of the crane's beak

3. The context of paragraphs 13-16, helps the reader know that *purblind* most likely means:
   a. Blind in one eye
   b. Blind in two eyes
   c. Old
   d. Trustworthy

4. Why did the crane agree to bring the crab to the pond?
   a. Because he always kept his word
   b. Because the crab asked him to
   c. Because the Genius told him to
   d. Because the crab threatened him

5. Which of these is the best summary of the selection?
   a. The pond that the fish live in is drying up, and the crane offers to take the fish to a pond with more water. The fish don't trust the crane, so they send a representative to check out the new pond. He says that the pond exists, so they all agree to go with the crane. The crane drops them off at the pond and then comes back to take the crab. The crab also doesn't trust the crane, but the crane is honest and also takes him to the pond.
   b. The pond that the fish live in is drying up, and the crane offers to take the fish to a pond with more water. The fish don't trust the crane, so they send a representative to check out the new pond. He says that the pond exists, so they all agree to go with the crane. Instead of taking the fish to the pond, the crane eats each one. He then goes back to the dry pond and offers to take the crab. The crab also doesn't trust the crane, but the crane is honest this time and takes him straight to the new pond.
   c. The pond that the fish live in is drying up, and the crane offers to take the fish to a pond with more water. The fish don't trust the crane, so they send a representative to check out the new pond. He says that the pond exists, so they all agree to go with the crane. Instead of taking the fish to the pond, the crane eats each one. He then goes back to the dry pond and offers to take the crab. The crab also doesn't trust the crane, so he creates a plan to force the crane to take him to the pond. Just when the crane is about to eat the crab, the crab attacks him. The crane quickly eats him up.
   d. The pond that the fish live in is drying up, and the crane offers to take the fish to a pond with more water. The fish don't trust the crane, so they send a representative to check out the new pond. He says that the pond exists, so they all agree to go with the crane. Instead of taking the fish to the pond, the crane eats each one. He then goes back to the dry pond and offers to take the crab. The crab also doesn't trust the crane, so he creates a plan to force the crane to take him to the pond. When the crane tries to veer away from the pond to eat the crab, the crab attacks him. The crane agrees to take the crab to the pond. When they get to the pond, the crab attacks the crane again.

6. The author organizes the story mainly by:
   a. introducing Bodisat and showing his role in the crane's story
   b. using cause and effect to show what happens when a pond runs dry
   c. telling a story and then giving a moral
   d. giving a moral and then telling a story that supports it

7. The author mentions Bodisat at the beginning and end of the story in order to show that
   a. Bodisat is the main character of the story
   b. the story is non-fiction
   c. the story is a fable
   d. the story is realistic fiction

- 48 -

8. In paragraph 6, what does the crane mean when he says, "I am sitting thinking about you."?
   a. That he's worried about the fish
   b. That he's worried about the crab
   c. That he's thinking of a way to trick the fish
   d. That he's thinking about the larger pond

9. How are the crane and the crab similar?
   a. They both live in water
   b. They both like to eat fish
   c. They are both deceitful
   d. They both enjoy each other's company

10. In paragraph 30, what proof does the crane present?
    a. The new pond is larger than the old pond
    b. He ate the fish
    c. He ate the crab
    d. The fish are stupid

11. What is the moral of this story?
    a. Villains succeed by being especially evil
    b. Villains succeed by tricking others
    c. Villains that are exceedingly clever are evil
    d. Villains prosper by their villainy

12. In paragraph 27, what does the phrase "blacksmith's pincers" show about the crab?
    a. That his claws close tightly
    b. That his claws are sharp
    c. That he wants to hurt the crane
    d. That he's excited to go to the pond

Questions 13 – 16 pertain to the following passage:

"Five Children and It" by E. Nesbit

(1) The house was three miles from the station, but, before the dusty hired hack had rattled along for five minutes, the children began to put their heads out of the carriage window and say, "Aren't we nearly there?" And every time they passed a house, which was not very often, they all said, "Oh, *is* this it?" But it never was, till they reached the very top of the hill, just past the chalk-quarry and before you come to the gravel-pit. And then there was a white house with a green garden and an orchard beyond, and mother said, "Here we are!"
(2) "How white the house is," said Robert.
(3) "And look at the roses," said Anthea.

(4) "And the plums," said Jane.

(5) "It is rather decent," Cyril admitted.

(6) The Baby said, "Wanty go walky;" and the hack stopped with a last rattle and jolt.

(7) Everyone got its legs kicked or its feet trodden on in the scramble to get out of the carriage that very minute, but no one seemed to mind. Mother, curiously enough, was in no hurry to get out; and even when she had come down slowly and by the step, and with no jump at all, she seemed to wish to see the boxes carried in, and even to pay the driver, instead of joining in that first glorious rush round the garden and orchard and the thorny, thistly, briery, brambly wilderness beyond the broken gate and the dry fountain at the side of the house. But the children were wiser, for once. It was not really a pretty house at all; it was quite ordinary, and mother thought it was rather inconvenient, and was quite annoyed at there being no shelves, to speak of, and hardly a cupboard in the place. Father used to say that the iron-work on the roof and coping was like an architect's nightmare. But the house was deep in the country, with no other house in sight, and the children had been in London for two years, without so much as once going to the seaside even for a day by an excursion train, and so the White House seemed to them a sort of Fairy Palace set down in an Earthly Paradise. For London is like prison for children, especially if their relations are not rich.

13. Read the sentence from paragraph 7: *But the children were wiser for once.* What are the children wise about?
    a. They know that the house is nicer than it looks
    b. They know the house is less nice than it looked at first glance
    c. They know that being at a house in the country will be better than being in London
    d. They know that the broken-down house will convince Mother to take them back to London

14. What phrase from the passage best shows the children's emotions when they arrive at the house?
    a. And then there was a white house with a green garden and an orchard beyond
    b. How white the house is
    c. Everyone got its legs kicked or its feet trodden on in the scramble to get out of the carriage
    d. It was not really a pretty house

15. Which of these best describes the selection?
    a. The children are moving into a new house in London after living in the country
    b. The children are moving into a new house in the country after living in London
    c. The children are moving to a house in a new country
    d. The children are moving from a prison to a fairy palace

- 50 -

16. What's the most logical reason why Mother was not in a hurry to get out of the carriage?

    a. She's unhappy to be moving into the new house

    b. She's excited to see the new house

    c. She does not want to explore with children

    d. She needs to help the driver

Questions 17 -21 pertain to the following passage:

"The Railway Children" by E. Nesbit

(1) "Wake up, dears. We're there."

(2) They woke up, cold and melancholy, and stood shivering on the draughty platform while the baggage was taken out of the train. Then the engine, puffing and blowing, set to work again, and dragged the train away. The children watched the tail-lights of the guard's van disappear into the darkness.

(3) This was the first train the children saw on that railway which was in time to become so very dear to them. They did not guess then how they would grow to love the railway, and how soon it would become the centre of their new life, nor what wonders and changes it would bring to them. They only shivered and sneezed and hoped the walk to the new house would not be long. Peter's nose was colder than he ever remembered it to have been before. Roberta's hat was crooked, and the elastic seemed tighter than usual. Phyllis's shoe-laces had come undone.

(4) "Come," said Mother, "we've got to walk. There aren't any cabs here."

(5) The walk was dark and muddy. The children stumbled a little on the rough road, and once Phyllis absently fell into a puddle, and was picked up damp and unhappy. There were no gas-lamps on the road, and the road was uphill. The cart went at a foot's pace, and they followed the gritty crunch of its wheels. As their eyes got used to the darkness, they could see the mound of boxes swaying dimly in front of them.

(6) A long gate had to be opened for the cart to pass through, and after that the road seemed to go across fields—and now it went down hill. Presently a great dark lumpish thing showed over to the right.

(7) "There's the house," said Mother. "I wonder why she's shut the shutters."

(8) "Who's SHE?" asked Roberta.

(9) "The woman I engaged to clean the place, and put the furniture straight and get supper."

(10) There was a low wall, and trees inside.

(11) "That's the garden," said Mother.

(12 "It looks more like a dripping-pan full of black cabbages," said Peter.

(13) The cart went on along by the garden wall, and round to the back of the house, and here it clattered into a cobble-stoned yard and stopped at the back door.

(14) There was no light in any of the windows.

(15) Everyone hammered at the door, but no one came.

(16) The man who drove the cart said he expected Mrs.Viney had gone home.

(17) "You see your train was that late," said he.

(18) "But she's got the key," said Mother. "What are we to do?"

(19) "Oh, she'll have left that under the doorstep," said the cart man; "folks do hereabouts." He took the lantern off his cart and stooped.

(20) "Ay, here it is, right enough," he said.

(21) He unlocked the door and went in and set his lantern on the table.

(22) "Got e'er a candle?" said he.

(23) "I don't know where anything is." Mother spoke rather less cheerfully than usual.

(24) He struck a match. There was a candle on the table, and he lighted it. By its thin little glimmer the children saw a large bare kitchen with a stone floor. There were no curtains, no hearth-rug. The kitchen table from home stood in the middle of the room. The chairs were in one corner, and the pots, pans, brooms, and crockery in another. There was no fire, and the black grate showed cold, dead ashes.

(25) As the cart man turned to go out after he had brought in the boxes, there was a rustling, scampering sound that seemed to come from inside the walls of the house.

(26) "Oh, what's that?" cried the girls.

(27) "It's only the rats," said the cart man. And he went away and shut the door, and the sudden draught of it blew out the candle.

(28) "Oh, dear," said Phyllis, "I wish we hadn't come!" and she knocked a chair over.

(29) "ONLY the rats!" said Peter, in the dark.

17. Which of these is NOT a reason why the walk to the house was difficult?
    a. The road was muddy
    b. There was not any light along the road
    c. The walk was long
    d. The road was not smooth

18. In paragraph 15, why did no one come to the door?
    a. Mrs. Viney was running an errand
    b. The train was late
    c. Mrs. Viney didn't hear the knocking
    d. The door was unlocked

19. Which state below best reflects the impression made in paragraph 24?
    a. The house is homey and cozy
    b. The house is not homey or cozy
    c. Mrs. Viney lit a fire to welcome the family
    d. The house is missing furniture

20. What can the reader conclude about the passage?
    a. The children are excited to arrive at the house
    b. The children love the train and railroad
    c. The family is friends with Mrs. Viney
    d. The children are seeing the house for the first time

21. Which sentence or phrase from the passage best illustrates why the author chose the story's title?
    a. The baggage was taken out of the train
    b. Then the engine, puffing and blowing
    c. The children watched the tail-lights of the guard's van disappear into the darkness
    d. Which in time was to become so very dear to them

Questions 22 – 25 pertain to both passages from "Five Children and It" and "The Railway Children"

22. What do the children in "Five Children and It" have in common with the children in "The Railway Children"?
    a. They are excited to move into their new house
    b. They are moving to an unfamiliar location
    c. They are disappointed when they see their new house
    d. They are eager to explore the country

23. Which sentence or phrase from "Five Children and It" shows that the mothers in both stories felt the same about the new house?
    a. The house was three miles from the station
    b. Mother said, "Here we are!"
    c. Mother, curiously enough, was in no hurry to get out
    d. But the house was deep in the country

24. What's the difference in the way the children in the two stories perceive their new houses?
    a. The children in "Five Children and It" feel like their new house is a prison, but the children in "The Railway Children" are excited to explore
    b. The children in "Five Children and It" feel like their new house is a prison, and the children in "The Railway Children" think their new house is run down
    c. The children in "Five Children and It" are disappointed that their new house seems run-down, but the children in "The Railway Children" think their new house is a wonderful as a fairy palace
    d. The children in "Five Children and It" think their new house is wonderful even though it's run down, but the children in "The Railway Children" are not excited about moving into a rundown house

25. Both passages are the beginning of longer works. What do these beginnings have in common?
    a. They place the characters in a new setting
    b. They place the characters in an uncomfortable situation
    c. They introduce the characters by describing their appearance and personality
    d. They foreshadow that the children in both stories will argue with their parents

Questions 26 – 37 pertain to the following passage:

A Child's History of England by Charles Dickens

(1) If you look at a Map of the World, you will see, in the left-hand upper corner of the Eastern Hemisphere, two Islands lying in the sea. They are England and Scotland, and Ireland. England and Scotland form the greater part of these Islands. Ireland is the next in size. The little neighbouring islands, which are so small upon the Map as to be mere dots, are chiefly little bits of Scotland,—broken off, I dare say, in the course of a great length of time, by the power of the restless water.

(2) In the old days, a long, long while ago..., these Islands were in the same place, and the stormy sea roared round them, just as it roars now. But the sea was not alive, then, with great ships and brave sailors, sailing to and from all parts of the world. It was very lonely. The Islands lay solitary, in the great expanse of water. The foaming waves dashed against their cliffs, and the bleak winds blew over their forests; but the winds and waves brought no adventurers to land upon the Islands, and the savage Islanders knew nothing of the rest of the world, and the rest of the world knew nothing of them.

(3) It is supposed that the Phoenicians, who were an ancient people, famous for carrying on trade, came in ships to these Islands, and found that they produced tin and lead; both very useful things, as you

- 54 -

know, and both produced to this very hour upon the sea-coast. The most celebrated tin mines in Cornwall are, still, close to the sea. One of them, which I have seen, is so close to it that it is hollowed out underneath the ocean; and the miners say, that in stormy weather, when they are at work down in that deep place, they can hear the noise of the waves thundering above their heads. So, the Phœnicians, coasting about the Islands, would come, without much difficulty, to where the tin and lead were.

(4) The Phœnicians traded with the Islanders for these metals, and gave the Islanders some other useful things in exchange. The Islanders were, at first, poor savages, going almost naked, or only dressed in the rough skins of beasts, and staining their bodies, as other savages do, with coloured earths and the juices of plants. But the Phœnicians, sailing over to the opposite coasts of France and Belgium, and saying to the people there, 'We have been to those white cliffs across the water, which you can see in fine weather, and from that country, which is called Britain, we bring this tin and lead,' tempted some of the French and Belgians to come over also. These people settled themselves on the south coast of England, which is now called Kent; and, although they were a rough people too, they taught the savage Britons some useful arts, and improved that part of the Islands. It is probable that other people came over from Spain to Ireland, and settled there.

(5) Thus, by little and little, strangers became mixed with the Islanders, and the savage Britons grew into a wild, bold people; almost savage, still, especially in the interior of the country away from the sea where the foreign settlers seldom went; but hardy, brave, and strong.

(6) The whole country was covered with forests, and swamps. The greater part of it was very misty and cold. There were no roads, no bridges, no streets, no houses that you would think deserving of the name. A town was nothing but a collection of straw-covered huts, hidden in a thick wood, with a ditch all round, and a low wall, made of mud, or the trunks of trees placed one upon another. The people planted little or no corn, but lived upon the flesh of their flocks and cattle. They made no coins, but used metal rings for money. They were clever in basket-work, as savage people often are; and they could make a coarse kind of cloth, and some very bad earthenware. But in building fortresses they were much more clever.

(7) They made boats of basket-work, covered with the skins of animals, but seldom, if ever, ventured far from the shore. They made swords, of copper mixed with tin; but, these swords were of an

awkward shape, and so soft that a heavy blow would bend one. They made light shields, short pointed daggers, and spears—which they jerked back after they had thrown them at an enemy, by a long strip of leather fastened to the stem. The butt-end was a rattle, to frighten an enemy's horse. The ancient Britons, being divided into as many as thirty or forty tribes, each commanded by its own little king, were constantly fighting with one another, as savage people usually do; and they always fought with these weapons.

26. According to the author, why did the ancient Britons frequently fight with each other?
    a. They had many weapons
    b. They disliked the Phoenicians
    c. There were no roads or bridges
    d. They were divided into many tribes

27. What is paragraph 2 mostly about?
    a. The Map of the World
    b. The two islands and what they looked like
    c. The two islands and the people who lived there
    d. The winds and waves that blew against the island

28. Which sentence or phrase best shows the impact the Phoenicians had on the ancient Britons?
    a. The Phoenicians traded with the Islanders
    b. But the Phoenicians, sailing over to the opposite coasts of France and Belgium
    c. These people settled themselves on the south Coast of England
    d. The savage Britons grew into a wild, bold people

29. The tone throughout the selection is
    a. humorous
    b. informative
    c. angry
    d. bored

30. Which sentence or phrase best expresses the isolation of the islands of England and Scotland and Ireland?
    a. Which are so small upon the Map as to be mere dots
    b. The Islands lay solitary, in the great expanse of water
    c. They can hear the noise of the waves thundering above their heads
    d. Thus, by little and little, strangers became mixed with the Islanders

31. This passage is part of a longer work. Where does this selection most likely fit into the longer work?
    a. The beginning of the entire work
    b. The middle of a chapter
    c. The end of a chapter
    d. The end of the entire work

32. Read this phrase from paragraph 7: *But seldom, if ever, ventured far from the shore*. Why does the author include this phrase?
    a. To show the ways in which the people used boats
    b. To highlight the irony of making boats
    c. To show where the people used weapons
    d. To explain why the people built fortresses

33. What most likely tempted the French and Belgians to come over to Britain?
    a. The white cliffs of Britain
    b. The fine weather
    c. The tin and lead
    d. Juices of plants

34. This passage is mostly likely to appear in a:
    a. Newspaper
    b. Travel book
    c. Textbook
    d. Novel

35. Look at the time line below:

Which answer choice shows the correct order of events?
    a. No change
    b. 1, 3, 2
    c. 2, 1 3
    d. 3, 1, 2

36. Why does the author begin the passage by describing a map?
   a. To explain the location of the islands
   b. To show the roads that run through England, Scotland, and Ireland
   c. To show how the little bits of Scotland broke away from the main island
   d. To show the size of the islands in relation to France and Belgium

37. What sentence or phrase best describes the lands in the interior of the islands (the parts away from the coast)?
   a. These people settled themselves on the south coast of England, which is now called Kent
   b. Especially in the interior of the country away from the sea where the foreign settlers seldom went
   c. The whole country was covered with forests and swamps.
   d. The ancient Britons, being divided into as many as thirty or forty tribes, each commanded by its own king

Questions 38 – 48 pertain to the following passage:

Ten Boys from Dickens
"The Boy Musician"

By Kate Dickinson Sweetser

(1) Johannes Chrysostemus Wolfgangus Theophilus Mozart—what a burden to be put upon a baby's tiny shoulders!
(2) If there is any truth underlying the belief that a name can in some measure foreshadow a child's future, then surely Wolfgang Mozart, who was born in Salzburg in 1756, came honestly by his heritage of greatness, for when he was only a day old he received the five-part name, to which was later added his confirmation name of Sigismundus. But as soon as he could choose for himself, the little son of Marianne and Leopold Mozart from his store of names, selected Wolfgang, to which he added Amadeus, by which combination he was always known, and the name is for ever linked with the memory of a great genius.
(3) Almost before he could talk plainly the little fellow showed himself to be a musical prodigy, and when he was scarcely three years old he would steal into the room where his father was giving a lesson on the harpsichord to Anna (or "Nannerl," as she was called), the sister five years older than himself, and while she was being taught, Wolfgang would listen and watch with breathless attention.
(4) One day when the lesson was over, he begged his father to teach him too, but Leopold Mozart only laughed as he answered, glancing down into the child's serious face looking so intently into his:
(5) "Wait, my little man, thou art but a baby yet. Wait awhile, my Wolferl!" and the disappointed little musician crept away, but as soon

as Nannerl and his father had left the room, the tiny fellow crept back again, went to the harpsichord and standing on tiptoe, touched the keys with his chubby fingers stretched wide apart until he reached and played *a perfect chord*! Leopold Mozart was in another part of the house, but his sensitive ear caught the sound, and he rushed back to find his baby on tiptoe before the harpsichord, giving the first hint of his marvellous ability.

(6) At once the proud and excited father began to give him lessons, and always, too, from that day, whenever Nannerl had her lesson, Wolfgang perched on his father's knee, and listened with rapt absorption, and often when the lesson was over, he would repeat what she had played in exact imitation of her manner of playing.

(7) Leopold Mozart, who was himself a talented musician, saw with pride almost beyond expression, that both of his children inherited his musical ability, and soon felt that Wolfgang was a genius. When the boy was only four, his father, to test his powers, tried to teach him some minuets which to his perfect astonishment, Wolfgang played after him in a most extraordinary manner, not merely striking the notes correctly, but marking the rhythm with accurate expression, and to learn and play each minuet the little fellow required only half an hour.

(8) When he was five years old, one day his father entered the sitting-room of their home and found Wolfgang bending over a table, writing so busily that he did not hear his father enter, or see that he was standing beside him. Wolfgang's chubby little hand held the pen awkwardly, but held it with firm determination while it travelled back and forth across a large sheet of paper on which he was scribbling a strange collection of hieroglyphics, with here and there a huge blot, testifying to his haste and inexperience in the use of ink.

(9) What was he trying to do? His father's curiosity finally overcame him and he asked:

(10) "What are you doing, Wolfgang?" The curly head was raised with an impatient gesture.

(11) "I am composing a concerto for the harpsichord. I have nearly finished the first part."

(12) "Let me see it."

(13) "No, please, I have not yet finished."

(14) But even as he spoke, the eager father had taken up the paper and carried it over to where a friend stood, and they looked it over together, exchanging amused glances at the queer characters on it. Presently Leopold Mozart, after looking carefully at it, said:

(15) "Why it really seems to be composed by rule! But it is so difficult that no one could ever play it."

(16) "Oh, yes, they could, but it must be studied first," exclaimed little Wolfgang eagerly, and running to the harpsichord, he added:

(17) "See, this is the way it begins," and he was able to play enough of it, to show what his idea in writing it had been, and his father and the friend who had before exchanged glances of amusement, now looked at each other with wonder not untouched with awe.

38. Why does Leopold Mozart refuse to teach Wolfgang how to play the harpsichord at first?
    a. He does not think Wolfgang has talent
    b. Wolfgang has already shown he is a musical genius
    c. He thinks Wolfgang is too young
    d. He only wanted Anna to learn harpsichord

39. This passage describes real people from history. Which aspect of the passage is most likely made up by the author?
    a. The names of Wolfgang and his family members
    b. The dialogue between Wolfgang and Leopold
    c. The age at which Wolfgang composed the concerto
    d. The speed with which Wolfgang learned to play minuets

40. Which sentence or phrase from the passage best helps the reader infer that Wolferl is a nickname for Wolfgang?
    a. Johannes Chrysostemus Wolfgangus Theophilus Mozart – what a burden to be put upon a baby's tiny shoulders!
    b. But as soon as he could choose for himself, the little son of Marianne and Leopold Mozart from his store of names, selected Wolfgang, to which he added Amadeus
    c. He would steal into the room where his father was giving a lesson on the harpsichord to Anna (or "Nannerl," as she was called), the sister five years older than himself
    d. "Wait, my little man, thou art but a baby yet."

41. In paragraph 5, Leopold says he does not want to teach Wolfgang harpsichord yet. What makes him change his mind?
    a. Anna asks him
    b. Wolfgang asks him
    c. Wolfgang plays a chord by himself
    d. Wolfgang composes a concerto

42. In paragraph 8, the phrase "a strange collection of hieroglyphics" most likely refers to
    a. letters in a foreign language
    b. pictures and shapes
    c. sentences and paragraphs
    d. music notes

43. How does Leopold feel after Wolfgang plays the beginning of the concerto?
    a. Amazed
    b. Amused
    c. Eager
    d. Awkward

44. What word in paragraph 4 best defines the word *intently*?
    a. Begged
    b. Laughed
    c. Serious
    d. Looking

45. What does the passage imply is the main reason for Wolfgang's musical skill?
    a. Talent
    b. Hard work
    c. His father's determination
    d. Hours of lessons

46. Based on the context of the passage, what is the meaning of the word *prodigy* as it is used in paragraph 3?
    a. Baby
    b. Genius
    c. Student
    d. Son

47. What is the most logical reason why Leopold wants Anna and Wolfgang to play the harpsichord?
    a. He wants his children to work hard
    b. He's also a musician
    c. He wants to impress his friends
    d. He knows Anna and Wolfgang love music and wants to please them

48. Look at the timeline below.

What event best fits in the missing arrow?
    a. Wolfgang plays a perfect chord on the harpsichord
    b. Wolfgang watches Anna's music lessons
    c. Wolfgang amazes Leopold's friend
    d. Wolfgang learns to play minuets in just a half hour

Answers and Explanations

1. B: The correct answer is B because the crab says in paragraph 24, "If this fellow once got hold of fish, he would never let them go in a pond." This sentence shows that the crab knows that he cannot trust the crane. Even thought the crab says in paragraph 22 that he's worried he'll fall, he needs to defend himself from the crane because he's worried the crane will eat him. Choice C is incorrect because the crab is not friends with the crane; in fact, he does not trust the crane and is worried the crane will attack him. Although the crab is glad to leave the dry pond for the wet pond, he's worried about being transported on the crane because he knows that the crane will probably try to eat him.

2. C: In paragraph 11, the fish say that they think the crane is hoping to eat them, one after the other. They know that cranes like to eat fish and don't want to get eaten. Choice A is incorrect because skeptical means to not trust someone. If the crane liked helping the fish out, the fish would not be skeptical of him. Choice B is incorrect because the crane is not making the water run dry. Instead, paragraph 2 says that the water used to run short at the dry season. Choice D is incorrect because it is the crab that is worried he will fall, not the fish.

3. A: The correct answer is choice A because paragraph 13 says that the fish was blind in one eye. Choice B is incorrect because the fish is blind in one eye, not two. While the passage does say that the fish is old, choice C is incorrect because the word *purblind* contains the root word *blind* and is probably related to not being able to see. While the other fish do trust the purblind fish, purblind is most likely related to the word *blind*.

4. D: Choice D is the correct answer because the crab threatens to cut the crane's head off in paragraph 30. Choice A is incorrect because the crane demonstrates several times in the story that he does not keep his word. Choice B is incorrect because the crane intends to eat the crab instead of taking him to the pond. He only agrees to take the crab when he is threatened and does not care if the crab asks him. Choice C is incorrect because the Genius is a passive character that observes the crane's actions but does not interfere by giving him directions.

5. D: While all of the answer choices contain correct parts of the story, only choice D is fully correct. Choice A is incorrect because the crane does not drop the fish off at the pond; he eats them instead. Choice B is incorrect because the crane does not take the crab straight to the pond. He tries to veer off to the tree to eat the crab and only goes to the pond when the crab threatens him. Choice C is incorrect because the crane does not eat the crab.

6. C: The correct answer is C because the author tells the story of the crane's trickery and then ends with a moral in verse. While the author does introduce Bodisat at the

beginning of the story, Choice A is incorrect because Bodisat does not have a role in the crane's story; he only observes. Choice B is incorrect because the pond running dry is not the reason why the fish were eaten; the crane's trickery is the cause. Choice D is incorrect because the moral is at the end of the story, not the beginning.

7. C: The correct answer is C because the mythical character of Bodisat and the moral at the end of the story show that the story is a fable. Choice A is incorrect because Bodisat is only mentioned at the beginning and end of the story; Bodisat observes the events but does not participate in them. Choice B is incorrect because the story does not display characteristics of non-fiction. For example, the animals speak, which cannot happen in a true story. Choice D is incorrect because realistic fiction portrays a made-up story that could happen in real life; since animals cannot talk in real life, the story cannot be realistic fiction.

8. C: The correct answer is C because the crane says in paragraph 3 that he wants to outwit the fish. Paragraph 5 says that the crane sat by the water and thought about how he should outwit the fish. Choice A is incorrect even though the crane pretends that he's worried about the fish. He pretends to worry about the fish so that he can convince them to go to the other pond. Therefore, he is lying in paragraph 8. Choice B is incorrect because the crane has not even met the crab in paragraph 6. Choice D is incorrect because the crane is lying in paragraph 10 when he talks about the large pond. He's really thinking about how he can trick the fish and find a way to eat them.

9. C: Choice C is the correct answer because both the crane and crab are deceitful, or tricky. The crane is deceitful when he tricks the fish and convinces them to let him take them to the pond. The crab is deceitful when he plans to attack the crane if the crane does not take him to the pond. Choice A is incorrect because only the crab lives in the water. The story does not say where the crane lives. Choice B is incorrect because the story does not say that the crab eats fish; in fact, the story doesn't say what the crab eats at all. Choice D is incorrect because the crane and crab are not friends. The crane wants to eat the crab.

10. B: The correct answer is B because the crane points out the fish bones underneath the Varana tree. Choice A is incorrect because the crane does not show proof that the pond is larger in paragraph 30; he shows the crab the pond in paragraph 27. Choice C is incorrect because the crane is talking to the crab in 27; he hasn't eaten the crab and can't show proof. Choice D is incorrect because the crab, not the crane, says that the fish are stupid.

11. B: The verse at the end of the story presents the moral and says villains won't prosper, or succeed, through villainy. Instead, villains win through deceit, or trickery. Choices A and D are incorrect because the moral says that villains don't succeed through villainy or evil. Choice C is incorrect because the moral does not say that clever villains are also evil. Instead, it says that the villain is clever.

12. A: The correct answer is A because the second sentence of paragraph 26 says that the crab caught hold of his neck securely, which also means tightly. Choice B is

incorrect because no adjectives in the paragraph show that the claws are sharp; instead, the claws are tight and very secure. While the crab does have plans to hurt the crane, choice C is incorrect because the phrase "blacksmith's pincers" simply shows how tightly and securely the crab is holding onto the crane. Choice D is incorrect because the shape of his claws does not show the crab's emotions; his claws do not change shape based on how he's feeling.

13. C: The correct answer is C because paragraph 7 says that the children consider the house to be like a Fairy Palace even though it "was not a pretty house at all". The children are wise because they are glad to be living in the country, since London was "like prison for children". Choice A is incorrect because the paragraph makes clear that the house is run down and not pretty. Despite its looks, the children still love the house. Although the house is less nice than it appeared at first glance, choice B is incorrect because the sentence "But the children were wiser for once" means that the children knew that they would love the house despite its run-down appearance. Choice D is incorrect because the children do not want to go back to London. They are excited to be living in the country and considered London to be like a prison.

14. C: Choice C is the correct answer because the sentence shows the eagerness the children felt when they arrived. There was a scramble to get out of the carriage because the children were so excited to explore the new house. Choice A is incorrect because the sentence simply describes the house and doesn't hint at emotions. Choice B is incorrect because it only show's Robert's awe that the house is so white; it doesn't show how all the children feel. Choice D is incorrect because the children were excited to explore even though the house wasn't pretty; this choice doesn't show the children's excitement or other emotions.

15. B: The correct answer is B because the new house is in the country and paragraph 7 says that the children had been in London for two years. Choice A is incorrect because it is the opposite of what happened in the story. Instead of moving to London, the children are moving to the country. Choice C is incorrect because the children are not moving to a new country; they are moving to the country, which is an area that is not near a city. Choice D is incorrect because the passage uses *prison* and *fairy palace* as metaphors. The children aren't moving from a literal prison to a real fairy palace. Instead, they're moving from a city that felt like a prison to a house that feels like a fairy palace.

16. A: The correct answer is choice A because Mother does not seem happy to move into the house. She does not join in the "glorious rush" and thinks that the house is "rather inconvenient". Choice B is incorrect because Mother's hesitation to see the new house shows that she's not excited. While it's true that mother does not seem to want to explore with the children, choice C is not as logical a reason as choice A. The main reason why Mother doesn't want to explore the house is because she is reluctant to move in. Choice D is incorrect because the passage does not indicate that the driver needs help. Instead, Mother watches him carry the boxes in and pays him. She does this instead of exploring because she is not excited to move in.

17. C: The correct answer is choice C because the passage does not say that the walk was long. The passage does say in paragraph 6 that the family had to open and pass through a long gate, but it does not say that it was a long walk. All of the other answer choices are supported by the passage. The first sentence of paragraph five says the walk was muddy and dark. Paragraph 5 also says there were no gas lamps on the road. The second sentence of paragraph five says that the road was rough, which means it was not smooth.

18. B: Choice B is the correct answer because the cart driver says that the train was late in paragraph 17. Choice A is incorrect; the cart driver says in paragraph 16 that Mrs. Viney has gone home, not that she's run an errand. Choice C is incorrect because Mrs. Viney wasn't in the house. Choice D is incorrect because the door was locked; the cart man fetched the key from under the doorstep in order to unlock it.

19. B: The correct answer is B because the details about the house show that it's neither homey nor cozy. For example, paragraph 24 says that there is a stone floor, no curtains, no hearth rug, no fire, and rats in the walls. Choice A is incorrect because the house is the opposite of homey and cozy. Choice C is incorrect because Mrs. Viney did not light a fire for the family; paragraph 24 says that the fireplace had "cold, dead ashes". Choice D is incorrect because there is furniture in the house. Paragraph 24 describes the kitchen table and chairs.

20. D: The correct answer is choice D because the cart man shows them the way to the house and is the only one who knows where the key is. The reader also knows that the children haven't been in this town before because paragraph 3 says that the train was the very first one they saw on the railway tracks. Choice A is incorrect because the children don't show excitement. They are tired and cold. Peter's observation that the garden looks like "dripping-pan full of black cabbages" shows that he and his siblings are not enchanted by the house. Choice B is incorrect because paragraph 3 makes it clear that the children will learn to love the railway but don't love it yet. Choice C is incorrect because paragraphs 8 and 9 make it clear that the family does not know Mrs. Viney. Roberta asks who Mrs. Viney is and Mother explains that she hired Mrs. Viney to clean the house.

21. D: The best answer is choice D because the surrounding context shows that the phrase is talking about the railway. Since the story is called "The Railway Children", it is logical that the children might get this name because they love the railway. Although the other choices mention the train, they don't illustrate the reason why the author chose the title "The Railway Children" because they don't show the children's feelings about the railway. Choice A simply describes the action of removing the baggage from the train, choice B describes the train's engine, and choice C describes the children watching the train chug away.

22. B: The correct answer is choice B because both children are moving to a new house that they don't seem to know anything about. Choices A and C are incorrect

because only the children in "Five Children and It" are excited when they see the house, and only the children in "The Railway Children" are disappointed. "Five Children and It" hints that the children are eager to explore the country in addition to the house, but choice D is also incorrect because the children in "The Railway Children" do not show this eagerness.

23. C: Choice C is the best answer because Mother in "Five Children and It" is not eager to see the new house and is not excited to move. Likewise, Mother in "The Railway Children" is also unhappy, as shown in paragraph 23 when she speaks "rather less cheerfully than usual". Choice A is incorrect because it states a fact rather than showing Mother's emotion. Choice B is incorrect because the words "Here we are" do not show Mother's state of mind; from these words, the reader cannot determine if mother is disappointed or excited to be at the house. Choice D is incorrect because it describes the house's location but doesn't show Mother's feelings.

24. D: Paragraph 7 in "Five Children and It" show that the children are very excited to explore their new house and are looking forward to living in the country. Many details from "The Railway Children" show that the children in that story are not excited about moving or their new house. For example, paragraph 2 says that they were melancholy and paragraph 12 describes the garden as a pan of black cabbages. Choices A and B are incorrect because the children in "Five Children and It" thought that living in London was like being in a prison; they don't feel the same way about their new house. Choice A is also incorrect because the children in "The Railway Children" are not excited to explore their new house; they seem reluctant to move. Choice C is incorrect because it's the children in "Five Children and It" that think the new house is wonderful. Likewise, the children in "The Railway Children" are the ones who are disappointed.

25. A: The correct answer is choice A because both families are moving to a new home in a new area, or setting. Choice B is incorrect because the children in "Five Children and It" don't seem uncomfortable; instead, they are very eager. Choice C is incorrect because the passages describe the houses in detail but don't focus on the characters. Although the children in "Five Children and It" don't feel the same way as Mother about the new house, nothing in the passages foreshadows an argument with the parents. The children seem to respect and get along with their mothers.

26. D: The correct answer is D because the author says in paragraph 7 that the ancient Britons were divided into many tribes, each of which had its own king. The author implies that these tribes fought among each other. While paragraph 7 also says the ancient Britons had many weapons, it doesn't say that the weapons were the reason that they fought. Instead, it simply says that they fought with the weapons. Choice B is incorrect because paragraph 7 says that the ancient Britons constantly fought. However, the passage stops discussing the Phoenicians after paragraph 4. Choice C is incorrect because paragraph 6 says that there were no roads or bridges. The author gives this detail in order to describe the land. This

- 66 -

detail does not support paragraph 7, which says the ancient Britons frequently fought.

27. B: The correct answer is B because paragraph 2 describes the natural details of the islands. For example, the paragraph describes the foaming waves, the cliffs, and the winds that blew over the forests. Choice A is incorrect because the map is discussed in paragraph 1, not paragraph 2. Choice C is incorrect because paragraph 2 only briefly mentions the people who lived on the islands. The author uses paragraphs 3-5 to give more details about the people who lived on the islands. Choice D is incorrect because the answer choice is only a portion of paragraph 2. The paragraph describes many natural features of the islands in addition to the winds and waves.

28. D: The correct answer is D because the word 'grew' shows that the ancient Britons changed after the Phoenicians arrived. Choice A is incorrect because the answer choice only shows something that the Phoenicians did with the Britons; however, it does not describe how the Britons changed. Choice B is incorrect because the sentence only talks about the Phoenicians and does not mention the ancient Britons. Choice C is incorrect because it refers to the French and Belgians who moved to the England; it does not mention the ancient Britons.

29. B: The author describes the history of the islands and gives informative details about the islands and the people who lived there in the past. Choice A is incorrect because the author does not make jokes during the article; instead, he simply describes facts. Choice C is incorrect because the author does not display anger or any other emotions; he simply describes facts. Choice D is incorrect because the author proves that he's very interested in the topic by giving many descriptive details. Therefore, he is the opposite of bored.

30. B: The word *solitary* refers to isolation, or being alone. Furthermore, the sentence says that the islands are alone in a great expanse of water, which shows that other lands do not surround the islands. Choice A is incorrect because the sentence only talks about the size of the small islands off Scotland. It does not talk about where the islands are in relation to other, bigger lands. Choice C is incorrect because it shows the islanders' relationship with the sea. However, it does not talk about the separation that the islanders have with other people. Choice D is incorrect because it shows the opposite of isolation; the sentence shows how the people who came to the islands (such as the French, Belgians, and Spanish) mixed with the ancient Britons.

31. A: The correct answer is choice A because paragraph 1 acts as an introductory passage. It starts by describing the islands on the map. Paragraph 2 moves into the earliest history of the islands. Later paragraphs describe the history as more and more groups of people came to them. Because of this organization, the passage best fits at the beginning of a longer work. The reader can infer that the author will

continue describing the history of Britain throughout the rest of the work. Choices B, C, and D are incorrect because the first paragraphs of the passage are introductory.

32. B: The correct answer is B because the first part of the sentence describes the boats that the ancient Britons built. However, the phrase "But seldom, if ever, ventured far from the shore" says that the boats didn't go far from shore. This implies that the boats may not have been used much. Choice A is incorrect because the phrase does not talk about specific ways that the ancient Britons used the boats. Even though the author describes weapons in the same paragraph, the phrase in the question focuses on the boats that the people made. The paragraph only moves onto weapons in the second sentence. Choice D is incorrect because the author does not connect the boats (discussed in paragraph 7) to the fortresses (discussed in at the end of paragraph 6).

33. C: Choice C is the best answer because paragraph 4 says that the tin and lead tempted some French and Belgian people to come over. Choice A is incorrect because 'white cliffs' are only mentioned by the Phoenicians when they are trying to explain to the French and Belgians where they have found the tin and lead. They point across the sea to the islands, using the white cliffs as a landmark. Choice B is incorrect because the fine weather was only mentioned as an example of when it is possible to see the cliffs. However, the weather was not mentioned as a way of convincing the French and Belgians to come over to the islands. Choice D is incorrect because the juices of plants were used by the islanders to paint their bodies.

34. C: The correct answer is C because the passage is informational and intended to teach children about the history of Britain. Choice A is incorrect because a newspaper is used to discuss current events and does not typically have long articles about history. While travel books sometimes have historical information, choice B is incorrect because the passage only talks about history. It does not describe the sites that travelers could expect to see. Choice D is incorrect because a novel is fictional, and this passage is non-fiction, or true.

35. D: The correct answer is choice D, as shown by paragraphs 3 and 4. The first sentence of paragraph 3 says that the Phoenicians found tin and lead on the islands. The first sentence of paragraph 4 says that the Phoenicians traded with the Islanders, who were also called the ancient Britons. Finally, the second-to-last sentence of paragraph 4 says that the French and Belgians settled in England. Choices A, B, and C are incorrect because they do not show the correct order that is described above.

36. A: Choice A is the best answer because paragraph 1 describes the location of the islands on the map. Readers know that they can find the islands by looking in the left-hand upper corner of the Eastern Hemisphere. Choice B is incorrect because paragraph six says that there were no roads that ran through England, Scotland, or Ireland during the time period that the passage is describing. Choice C is incorrect because the details about the small islands are only a small portion of the first

paragraph. Most of the paragraph describes how the islands appear on the map. Choice D is incorrect because the paragraph does not mention the size of the main islands. Furthermore, the paragraph does not mention France or Belgium; these countries are first mentioned in paragraph 4.

37. C: Choice C is the correct answer because this answer choice describes the lands by mentioning swamps and forests. Choice A is incorrect because it does not give details of the lands and also does not mention the interior of the islands, which is first mentioned in paragraph 5. While choice B mentions the interior, it is incorrect because it only says that it is away from the sea. It does not give details about the lands. Choice D is incorrect because it discusses the dynamics of the tribes and the relationships between the people rather than the features of the lands, such as the swamps and forests.

38. C: The best answer is choice C because Leopold calls Wolfgang a baby in paragraph 5. He then tells Wolfgang to wait awhile, meaning that he will teach Wolfgang harpsichord when he is older. Choice A is incorrect because Leopold does not yet know that Wolfgang is talented. He only discovers that Wolfgang is talented after he plays the perfect chord in paragraph 5. Choice B is incorrect because Wolfgang first shows his talent in paragraph 5. Leopold does not realize that Wolfgang is a musical genius until paragraph 7, which is after Wolfgang has been taking lessons for some time. Choice D is incorrect because Leopold clearly implies in paragraph 5 that he plans on teaching Wolfgang harpsichord when he is older.

39. B: While it's possible that someone recorded the exact dialogue between Wolfgang and Leopold, it is more likely that the author invented it in order to tell a story. Since this scene took place in front of few witnesses who could remember the words and because there are no recording devices, it's unlikely that the exact words of the dialogue are true. Choice A is incorrect because the author should have been able to find the exact names of Wolfgang and his family members through historical research. Choice C is incorrect because it's logical that Wolfgang and his father might remember the exact age that Wolfgang wrote a concerto, which would be considered a huge accomplishment worth remembering. It is more likely that the dialogue is made up because the many words of dialogue would be more difficult to remember than Wolfgang's age. Choice D is incorrect because Leopold likely remembered how quickly Wolfgang learned due to his being very proud of him.

40. C: The correct answer is C because the sentence gives Anna's name and then gives her nickname, Nannerl, in parentheses. The nickname Nannerl is in the same form as Wolferl (-erl at the end). This detail helps the reader understand that Wolferl is Wolfgang's nickname. Choice A is incorrect because the sentence simply gives five of Wolfgang's names. Although one of the names is Wolfgangus, the reader doesn't yet know that Wolfgang's father is likely to abbreviate Wolfgang with the –erl ending. Although choice B also includes Wolfgang's name, it is incorrect because it does not show the types of nicknames used in Wolfgang's time. Choice D is

incorrect because it does not give Wolfgang's name or explain how it is shortened into a nickname.

41. C: The correct answer is C because paragraph 5 shows that Wolfgang plays a chord by himself. The author emphasizes this feat by italicizing the words "perfect chord". Choice A is incorrect because Anna does not speak or ask anything at any point in the passage. Choice B is incorrect because Wolfgang does not *ask* his father to learn harpsichord. Instead, he comes into the lesson and shows his father that he wants to learn harpsichord by giving him a serious look (paragraph 4). Choice D is incorrect because Wolfgang composes the concerto in paragraphs 8-17, which is after he has already started taking harpsichord lessons.

42. D: Although hieroglyphics typically refers to letters in ancient Egyptian, they refer to music notes in this passage. It is clear that the 'hieroglyphics' refer to music notes in paragraph 11 when Wolfgang says that he is composing a concerto for the harpsichord. Choice A is incorrect because the word 'hieroglyphics' in paragraph 8 does not refer to the usual definition. While hieroglyphics are often made up of pictures and shapes, choice B is incorrect because they refer to the music notes used to compose the concerto. Choice C is incorrect because Wolfgang is composing or writing a concerto, not an essay.

43. A: The correct answer is choice A because paragraph 17 says "now looked at each other with wonder not untouched with awe." The words *wonder* and *awe* are synonymous with *amazed*. Although the passage says that Leopold and his friend exchanged amused glances (paragraphs 14 and 17), choice B is incorrect because they did not stay amused once they heard the concerto. Choice C is incorrect because Leopold was eager before he heard the concerto. Paragraph 14 says that he eagerly picked up Wolfgang's concerto to look at the music notes. Choice D is incorrect because the passage does not say that Leopold felt awkward or uncomfortable. Although paragraph 17 uses the similar-sounding word *awe*, this means wonder or amazement, not awkwardness.

44. C: The correct answer is C because the paragraph says "glancing down into the child's serious face". This phrase defines the word *intently* as *serious*. While it's true that Wolfgang begs his father for harpsichord lessons, the word *intently* refers to the serious look on Wolfgang's face and not the words he used when he asked for harpsichord lessons. Choice B is incorrect because *intently* refers to the look on Wolfgang's face, but the paragraph says that Leopold laughed. Therefore, Leopold was amused, not Wolfgang. Choice D is incorrect because *looking* is a verb that indicates what Wolfgang is doing. The word *intently* is an adverb that modifies the verb and shows how Wolfgang was looking at his father.

45. A: Although all the answer choices contributed to Wolfgang's abilities the best answer is choice A because the passage shows that his talent was the main reason for his success. The passage says several times that Wolfgang was a musical genius, or very talented, and that he had a lot of musical ability. Other parts of the passage,

such as paragraph 7, show that Wolfgang was able to play the harpsichord without much work at a very young age. Choices B, C, and D are incorrect because these three options supplemented Wolfgang's extraordinary talent but were not the main reason for his skill with music.

46. B: Although paragraph 3 does not use the word *genius*, the passage frequently refers to Wolfgang as a musical genius. For example, paragraph 2 calls him a "great genius". Choice A is incorrect because the word *prodigy* refers to Wolfgang's skill rather than his age. The paragraph talks about the things he was doing despite his age; these feats made him a prodigy, or genius. Choice C is incorrect because Wolfgang is not yet a music student. In fact, he would like to be a music student, but his father says in paragraph 5 that Wolfgang is too young for music lessons. Choice D is incorrect because the word *prodigy* does not refer to Wolfgang's relationship to his father. The adjective *musical* indicates that *prodigy* refers to Wolfgang's music ability.

47. B: Choice B is the best answer because the paragraph 7 says that Leopold was a talented musician. It also says that he was very proud that both of his children had musical talent. Although Leopold may have given Anna and Wolfgang a lot of work during music lessons, choice A is incorrect because it's not the most logical reason Leopold taught his children the harpsichord. If he simply wanted them to work hard, he could have engaged them in other activities. Choice C is incorrect because it is more logical that Leopold wants his children to excel in something that he also enjoys. Being able to impress his friends is an added bonus but not Leopold's main reason in teaching his children to play the harpsichord. Choice D is incorrect because nothing in the passage indicates that Leopold wants to please his children. Instead, paragraph 7 refers to Leopold's own musical abilities.

48. D: The passage describes Wolfgang's lessons in paragraph 6 and introduces the concerto in paragraph 8. The paragraph in between, paragraph 7, says that Wolfgang was able to learn minuets in under a half hour. Choice A is incorrect because Wolfgang played a perfect chord on the harpsichord the very first time he played the harpsichord, which happens in the first arrow. Choice B is incorrect because Wolfgang watches Anna's music lessons in paragraph 3, before he plays the harpsichord for the first time. Choice C is incorrect because Wolfgang amazes Leopold's friend in paragraph 17, after he writes the concerto.

Secret Key #1 - Time is Your Greatest Enemy

Pace Yourself

Wear a watch. At the beginning of the test, check the time (or start a chronometer on your watch to count the minutes), and check the time after every few questions to make sure you are "on schedule."

If you are forced to speed up, do it efficiently. Usually one or more answer choices can be eliminated without too much difficulty. Above all, don't panic. Don't speed up and just begin guessing at random choices. By pacing yourself, and continually monitoring your progress against your watch, you will always know exactly how far ahead or behind you are with your available time. If you find that you are one minute behind on the test, don't skip one question without spending any time on it, just to catch back up. Take 15 fewer seconds on the next four questions, and after four questions you'll have caught back up. Once you catch back up, you can continue working each problem at your normal pace.

Furthermore, don't dwell on the problems that you were rushed on. If a problem was taking up too much time and you made a hurried guess, it must be difficult. The difficult questions are the ones you are most likely to miss anyway, so it isn't a big loss. It is better to end with more time than you need than to run out of time.

Lastly, sometimes it is beneficial to slow down if you are constantly getting ahead of time. You are always more likely to catch a careless mistake by working more slowly than quickly, and among very high-scoring test takers (those who are likely to have lots of time left over), careless errors affect the score more than mastery of material.

Secret Key #2 - Guessing is not Guesswork

You probably know that guessing is a good idea. Unlike other standardized tests, there is no penalty for getting a wrong answer. Even if you have no idea about a question, you still have a 20-25% chance of getting it right.

Most test takers do not understand the impact that proper guessing can have on their score. Unless you score extremely high, guessing will significantly contribute to your final score.

Monkeys Take the Test

What most test takers don't realize is that to insure that 20-25% chance, you have to guess randomly. If you put 20 monkeys in a room to take this test, assuming they answered once per question and behaved themselves, on average they would get 20-25% of the questions correct. Put 20 test takers in the room, and the average will be much lower among guessed questions. Why?

1. The test writers intentionally write deceptive answer choices that "look" right. A test taker has no idea about a question, so he picks the "best looking" answer, which is often wrong. The monkey has no idea what looks good and what doesn't, so it will consistently be right about 20-25% of the time.
2. Test takers will eliminate answer choices from the guessing pool based on a hunch or intuition. Simple but correct answers often get excluded, leaving a 0% chance of being correct. The monkey has no clue, and often gets lucky with the best choice.

This is why the process of elimination endorsed by most test courses is flawed and detrimental to your performance. Test takers don't guess; they make an ignorant stab in the dark that is usually worse than random.

$5 Challenge

Let me introduce one of the most valuable ideas of this course—the $5 challenge:
- *You only mark your "best guess" if you are willing to bet $5 on it.*
- *You only eliminate choices from guessing if you are willing to bet $5 on it.*

Why $5? Five dollars is an amount of money that is small yet not insignificant, and can really add up fast (20 questions could cost you $100). Likewise, each answer choice on one question of the test will have a small impact on your overall score, but it can really add up to a lot of points in the end.

The process of elimination IS valuable. The following shows your chance of guessing it right:

If you eliminate wrong answer choices until only this many remain:	Chance of getting it correct:
1	100%
2	50%
3	33%

However, if you accidentally eliminate the right answer or go on a hunch for an incorrect answer, your chances drop dramatically—to 0%. By guessing among all the answer choices, you are GUARANTEED to have a shot at the right answer.

That's why the $5 test is so valuable. If you give up the advantage and safety of a pure guess, it had better be worth the risk.

What we still haven't covered is how to be sure that whatever guess you make is truly random. Here's the easiest way:
- *Always pick the first answer choice among those remaining.*

Such a technique means that you have decided, **before you see a single test question**, exactly how you are going to guess, and since the order of choices tells you nothing about which one is correct, this guessing technique is perfectly random.

This section is not meant to scare you away from making educated guesses or eliminating choices; you just need to define when a choice is worth eliminating. The $5 test, along with a pre-defined random guessing strategy, is the best way to make sure you reap all of the benefits of guessing.

Secret Key #3 - Practice Smarter, Not Harder

Many test takers delay the test preparation process because they dread the awful amounts of practice time they think necessary to succeed on the test. We have refined an effective method that will take you only a fraction of the time.

There are a number of "obstacles" in the path to success. Among these are answering questions, finishing in time, and mastering test-taking strategies. All must be executed on the day of the test at peak performance, or your score will suffer. The test is a mental marathon that has a large impact on your future.

Just like a marathon runner, it is important to work your way up to the full challenge. So first you just worry about questions, and then time, and finally strategy:

Success Strategy

1. Find a good source for practice tests.
2. If you are willing to make a larger time investment, consider using more than one study guide. Often the different approaches of multiple authors will help you "get" difficult concepts.
3. Take a practice test with no time constraints, with all study helps, "open book." Take your time with questions and focus on applying strategies.
4. Take a practice test with time constraints, with all guides, "open book."
5. Take a final practice test without open material and with time limits.

If you have time to take more practice tests, just repeat step 5. By gradually exposing yourself to the full rigors of the test environment, you will condition your mind to the stress of test day and maximize your success.

Secret Key #4 - Prepare, Don't Procrastinate

Let me state an obvious fact: if you take the test three times, you will probably get three different scores. This is due to the way you feel on test day, the level of preparedness you have, and the version of the test you see. Despite the test writers' claims to the contrary, some versions of the test WILL be easier for you than others.

Since your future depends so much on your score, you should maximize your chances of success. In order to maximize the likelihood of success, you've got to prepare in advance. This means taking practice tests and spending time learning the information and test taking strategies you will need to succeed.

Never go take the actual test as a "practice" test, expecting that you can just take it again if you need to. Take all the practice tests you can on your own, but when you go to take the official test, be prepared, be focused, and do your best the first time!

Secret Key #5 - Test Yourself

Everyone knows that time is money. There is no need to spend too much of your time or too little of your time preparing for the test. You should only spend as much of your precious time preparing as is necessary for you to get the score you need.

Once you have taken a practice test under real conditions of time constraints, then you will know if you are ready for the test or not.

If you have scored extremely high the first time that you take the practice test, then there is not much point in spending countless hours studying. You are already there.

Benchmark your abilities by retaking practice tests and seeing how much you have improved. Once you consistently score high enough to guarantee success, then you are ready.

If you have scored well below where you need, then knuckle down and begin studying in earnest. Check your improvement regularly through the use of practice tests under real conditions. Above all, don't worry, panic, or give up. The key is perseverance!

Then, when you go to take the test, remain confident and remember how well you did on the practice tests. If you can score high enough on a practice test, then you can do the same on the real thing.

General Strategies

The most important thing you can do is to ignore your fears and jump into the test immediately. Do not be overwhelmed by any strange-sounding terms. You have to jump into the test like jumping into a pool—all at once is the easiest way.

Make Predictions

As you read and understand the question, try to guess what the answer will be. Remember that several of the answer choices are wrong, and once you begin reading them, your mind will immediately become cluttered with answer choices designed to throw you off. Your mind is typically the most focused immediately after you have read the question and digested its contents. If you can, try to predict what the correct answer will be. You may be surprised at what you can predict.

Quickly scan the choices and see if your prediction is in the listed answer choices. If it is, then you can be quite confident that you have the right answer. It still won't hurt to check the other answer choices, but most of the time, you've got it!

Answer the Question

It may seem obvious to only pick answer choices that answer the question, but the test writers can create some excellent answer choices that are wrong. Don't pick an answer just because it sounds right, or you believe it to be true. It MUST answer the question. Once you've made your selection, always go back and check it against the question and make sure that you didn't misread the question and that the answer choice does answer the question posed.

Benchmark

After you read the first answer choice, decide if you think it sounds correct or not. If it doesn't, move on to the next answer choice. If it does, mentally mark that answer choice. This doesn't mean that you've definitely selected it as your answer choice, it just means that it's the best you've seen thus far. Go ahead and read the next choice. If the next choice is worse than the one you've already selected, keep going to the next answer choice. If the next choice is better than the choice you've already selected, mentally mark the new answer choice as your best guess.

The first answer choice that you select becomes your standard. Every other answer choice must be benchmarked against that standard. That choice is correct until proven otherwise by another answer choice beating it out. Once you've decided that no other answer choice seems as good, do one final check to ensure that your answer choice answers the question posed.

Valid Information

Don't discount any of the information provided in the question. Every piece of information may be necessary to determine the correct answer. None of the information in the question is there to throw you off (while the answer choices will certainly have information to throw you off). If two seemingly unrelated topics are discussed, don't ignore either. You can be confident there is a relationship, or it wouldn't be included in the question, and you are probably going to have to determine what is that relationship to find the answer.

Avoid "Fact Traps"

Don't get distracted by a choice that is factually true. Your search is for the answer that answers the question. Stay focused and don't fall for an answer that is true but irrelevant. Always go back to the question and make sure you're choosing an answer that actually answers the question and is not just a true statement. An answer can be factually correct, but it MUST answer the question asked. Additionally, two answers can both be seemingly correct, so be sure to read all of the answer choices, and make sure that you get the one that BEST answers the question.

Milk the Question

Some of the questions may throw you completely off. They might deal with a subject you have not been exposed to, or one that you haven't reviewed in years. While your lack of knowledge about the subject will be a hindrance, the question itself can give you many clues that will help you find the correct answer. Read the question carefully and look for clues. Watch particularly for adjectives and nouns describing difficult terms or words that you don't recognize. Regardless of whether you completely understand a word or not, replacing it with a synonym, either provided or one you more familiar with, may help you to understand what the questions are asking. Rather than wracking your mind about specific detailed information concerning a difficult term or word, try to use mental substitutes that are easier to understand.

The Trap of Familiarity

Don't just choose a word because you recognize it. On difficult questions, you may not recognize a number of words in the answer choices. The test writers don't put "make-believe" words on the test, so don't think that just because you only recognize all the words in one answer choice that that answer choice must be correct. If you only recognize words in one answer choice, then focus on that one. Is it correct? Try your best to determine if it is correct. If it is, that's great. If not, eliminate it. Each word and answer choice you eliminate increases your chances of getting the question correct, even if you then have to guess among the unfamiliar choices.

Eliminate Answers

Eliminate choices as soon as you realize they are wrong. But be careful! Make sure you consider all of the possible answer choices. Just because one appears right, doesn't mean that the next one won't be even better! The test writers will usually put more than one good answer choice for every question, so read all of them. Don't worry if you are stuck between two that seem right. By getting down to just two remaining possible choices, your odds are now 50/50. Rather than wasting too much time, play the odds. You are guessing, but guessing wisely because you've been able to knock out some of the answer choices that you know are wrong. If you are eliminating choices and realize that the last answer choice you are left with is also obviously wrong, don't panic. Start over and consider each choice again. There may easily be something that you missed the first time and will realize on the second pass.

Tough Questions

If you are stumped on a problem or it appears too hard or too difficult, don't waste time. Move on! Remember though, if you can quickly check for obviously incorrect answer choices, your chances of guessing correctly are greatly improved. Before you completely give up, at least try to knock out a couple of possible answers. Eliminate what you can and then guess at the remaining answer choices before moving on.

Brainstorm

If you get stuck on a difficult question, spend a few seconds quickly brainstorming. Run through the complete list of possible answer choices. Look at each choice and ask yourself, "Could this answer the question satisfactorily?" Go through each answer choice and consider it independently of the others. By systematically going through all possibilities, you may find something that you would otherwise overlook. Remember though that when you get stuck, it's important to try to keep moving.

Read Carefully

Understand the problem. Read the question and answer choices carefully. Don't miss the question because you misread the terms. You have plenty of time to read each question thoroughly and make sure you understand what is being asked. Yet a happy medium must be attained, so don't waste too much time. You must read carefully, but efficiently.

Face Value

When in doubt, use common sense. Always accept the situation in the problem at face value. Don't read too much into it. These problems will not require you to make huge leaps of logic. The test writers aren't trying to throw you off with a cheap trick. If you have to go beyond creativity and make a leap of logic in order to have an answer choice answer the question, then you should look at the other answer choices. Don't overcomplicate the problem by creating theoretical relationships or explanations that will warp time or space. These are normal problems rooted in reality. It's just that the applicable relationship or explanation may not be readily apparent and you have to figure things out. Use your common sense to interpret anything that isn't clear.

Prefixes

If you're having trouble with a word in the question or answer choices, try dissecting it. Take advantage of every clue that the word might include. Prefixes and suffixes can be a huge help. Usually they allow you to determine a basic meaning. Pre- means before, post- means after, pro - is positive, de- is negative. From these prefixes and suffixes, you can get an idea of the general meaning of the word and try to put it into context. Beware though of any traps. Just because con- is the opposite of pro-, doesn't necessarily mean congress is the opposite of progress!

Hedge Phrases

Watch out for critical hedge phrases, led off with words such as "likely," "may," "can," "sometimes," "often," "almost," "mostly," "usually," "generally," "rarely," and "sometimes." Question writers insert these hedge phrases to cover every possibility. Often an answer choice will be wrong simply because it leaves no room for exception. Unless the situation calls for them, avoid answer choices that have definitive words like "exactly," and "always."

Switchback Words

Stay alert for "switchbacks." These are the words and phrases frequently used to alert you to shifts in thought. The most common switchback word is "but." Others include "although," "however," "nevertheless," "on the other hand," "even though," "while," "in spite of," "despite," and "regardless of."

New Information

Correct answer choices will rarely have completely new information included. Answer choices typically are straightforward reflections of the material asked about and will directly relate to the question. If a new piece of information is included in an answer choice that doesn't even seem to relate to the topic being asked about, then that answer choice is likely incorrect. All of the information needed to answer the question is usually provided for you in the question. You should not have to make guesses that are unsupported or choose answer choices that require unknown information that cannot be reasoned from what is given.

Time Management

On technical questions, don't get lost on the technical terms. Don't spend too much time on any one question. If you don't know what a term means, then odds are you aren't going to get much further since you don't have a dictionary. You should be able to immediately recognize whether or not you know a term. If you don't, work with the other clues that you have—the other answer choices and terms provided— but don't waste too much time trying to figure out a difficult term that you don't know.

Contextual Clues

Look for contextual clues. An answer can be right but not the correct answer. The contextual clues will help you find the answer that is most right and is correct. Understand the context in which a phrase or statement is made. This will help you make important distinctions.

Don't Panic

Panicking will not answer any questions for you; therefore, it isn't helpful. When you first see the question, if your mind goes blank, take a deep breath. Force yourself to mechanically go through the steps of solving the problem using the strategies you've learned.

Pace Yourself

Don't get clock fever. It's easy to be overwhelmed when you're looking at a page full of questions, your mind is full of random thoughts and feeling confused, and the clock is ticking down faster than you would like. Calm down and maintain the pace that you have set for yourself. As long as you are on track by monitoring your pace, you are guaranteed to have enough time for yourself. When you get to the last few minutes of the test, it may seem like you won't have enough time left, but if you only have as many questions as you should have left at that point, then you're right on track!

Answer Selection

The best way to pick an answer choice is to eliminate all of those that are wrong, until only one is left and confirm that is the correct answer. Sometimes though, an answer choice may immediately look right. Be careful! Take a second to make sure that the other choices are not equally obvious. Don't make a hasty mistake. There are only two times that you should stop before checking other answers. First is when you are positive that the answer choice you have selected is correct. Second is when time is almost out and you have to make a quick guess!

Check Your Work

Since you will probably not know every term listed and the answer to every question, it is important that you get credit for the ones that you do know. Don't miss any questions through careless mistakes. If at all possible, try to take a second to look back over your answer selection and make sure you've selected the correct answer choice and haven't made a costly careless mistake (such as marking an answer choice that you didn't mean to mark). The time it takes for this quick double check should more than pay for itself in caught mistakes.

Beware of Directly Quoted Answers

Sometimes an answer choice will repeat word for word a portion of the question or reference section. However, beware of such exact duplication. It may be a trap! More than likely, the correct choice will paraphrase or summarize a point, rather than being exactly the same wording.

Slang

Scientific sounding answers are better than slang ones. An answer choice that begins "To compare the outcomes..." is much more likely to be correct than one that begins "Because some people insisted..."

Extreme Statements

Avoid wild answers that throw out highly controversial ideas that are proclaimed as established fact. An answer choice that states the "process should used in certain situations, if..." is much more likely to be correct than one that states the "process should be discontinued completely." The first is a calm rational statement and doesn't even make a definitive, uncompromising stance, using a hedge word "if" to provide wiggle room, whereas the second choice is a radical idea and far more extreme.

Answer Choice Families

When you have two or more answer choices that are direct opposites or parallels, one of them is usually the correct answer. For instance, if one answer choice states "x increases" and another answer choice states "x decreases" or "y increases," then those two or three answer choices are very similar in construction and fall into the same family of answer choices. A family of answer choices consists of two or three answer choices, very similar in construction, but often with directly opposite meanings. Usually the correct answer choice will be in that family of answer choices. The "odd man out" or answer choice that doesn't seem to fit the parallel construction of the other answer choices is more likely to be incorrect.

Special Report: How to Overcome Test Anxiety

The very nature of tests caters to some level of anxiety, nervousness, or tension, just as we feel for any important event that occurs in our lives. A little bit of anxiety or nervousness can be a good thing. It helps us with motivation, and makes achievement just that much sweeter. However, too much anxiety can be a problem, especially if it hinders our ability to function and perform.

"Test anxiety," is the term that refers to the emotional reactions that some test-takers experience when faced with a test or exam. Having a fear of testing and exams is based upon a rational fear, since the test-taker's performance can shape the course of an academic career. Nevertheless, experiencing excessive fear of examinations will only interfere with the test-taker's ability to perform and chance to be successful.

There are a large variety of causes that can contribute to the development and sensation of test anxiety. These include, but are not limited to, lack of preparation and worrying about issues surrounding the test.

Lack of Preparation

Lack of preparation can be identified by the following behaviors or situations:
- Not scheduling enough time to study, and therefore cramming the night before the test or exam
- Managing time poorly, to create the sensation that there is not enough time to do everything
- Failing to organize the text information in advance, so that the study material consists of the entire text and not simply the pertinent information
- Poor overall studying habits

Worrying, on the other hand, can be related to both the test taker, or many other factors around him/her that will be affected by the results of the test. These include worrying about:
- Previous performances on similar exams, or exams in general
- How friends and other students are achieving
- The negative consequences that will result from a poor grade or failure

There are three primary elements to test anxiety. Physical components, which involve the same typical bodily reactions as those to acute anxiety (to be discussed below). Emotional factors have to do with fear or panic. Mental or cognitive issues concerning attention spans and memory abilities.

Physical Signals

There are many different symptoms of test anxiety, and these are not limited to mental and emotional strain. Frequently there are a range of physical signals that will let a test taker know that he/she is suffering from test anxiety. These bodily changes can include the following:

- Perspiring
- Sweaty palms
- Wet, trembling hands
- Nausea
- Dry mouth
- A knot in the stomach
- Headache
- Faintness
- Muscle tension
- Aching shoulders, back and neck
- Rapid heart beat
- Feeling too hot/cold

To recognize the sensation of test anxiety, a test-taker should monitor him/herself for the following sensations:

- The physical distress symptoms as listed above
- Emotional sensitivity, expressing emotional feelings such as the need to cry or laugh too much, or a sensation of anger or helplessness
- A decreased ability to think, causing the test-taker to blank out or have racing thoughts that are hard to organize or control.

Though most students will feel some level of anxiety when faced with a test or exam, the majority can cope with that anxiety and maintain it at a manageable level. However, those who cannot are faced with a very real and very serious condition, which can and should be controlled for the immeasurable benefit of this sufferer.

Naturally, these sensations lead to negative results for the testing experience. The most common effects of test anxiety have to do with nervousness and mental blocking.

Nervousness

Nervousness can appear in several different levels:

- The test-taker's difficulty, or even inability to read and understand the questions on the test
- The difficulty or inability to organize thoughts to a coherent form

- The difficulty or inability to recall key words and concepts relating to the testing questions (especially essays)
- The receipt of poor grades on a test, though the test material was well known by the test taker

Conversely, a person may also experience mental blocking, which involves:
- Blanking out on test questions
- Only remembering the correct answers to the questions when the test has already finished.

Fortunately for test anxiety sufferers, beating these feelings, to a large degree, has to do with proper preparation. When a test taker has a feeling of preparedness, then anxiety will be dramatically lessened.

The first step to resolving anxiety issues is to distinguish which of the two types of anxiety are being suffered. If the anxiety is a direct result of a lack of preparation, this should be considered a normal reaction, and the anxiety level (as opposed to the test results) shouldn't be anything to worry about. However, if, when adequately prepared, the test-taker still panics, blanks out, or seems to overreact, this is not a fully rational reaction. While this can be considered normal too, there are many ways to combat and overcome these effects.

Remember that anxiety cannot be entirely eliminated, however, there are ways to minimize it, to make the anxiety easier to manage. Preparation is one of the best ways to minimize test anxiety. Therefore the following techniques are wise in order to best fight off any anxiety that may want to build.

To begin with, try to avoid cramming before a test, whenever it is possible. By trying to memorize an entire term's worth of information in one day, you'll be shocking your system, and not giving yourself a very good chance to absorb the information. This is an easy path to anxiety, so for those who suffer from test anxiety, cramming should not even be considered an option.

Instead of cramming, work throughout the semester to combine all of the material which is presented throughout the semester, and work on it gradually as the course goes by, making sure to master the main concepts first, leaving minor details for a week or so before the test.

To study for the upcoming exam, be sure to pose questions that may be on the examination, to gauge the ability to answer them by integrating the ideas from your texts, notes and lectures, as well as any supplementary readings.

If it is truly impossible to cover all of the information that was covered in that particular term, concentrate on the most important portions, that can be covered very well. Learn these concepts as best as possible, so that when the test comes, a goal can be made to use these concepts as presentations of your knowledge.

In addition to study habits, changes in attitude are critical to beating a struggle with test anxiety. In fact, an improvement of the perspective over the entire test-taking experience can actually help a test taker to enjoy studying and therefore improve the overall experience. Be certain not to overemphasize the significance of the grade - know that the result of the test is neither a reflection of self worth, nor is it a measure of intelligence; one grade will not predict a person's future success.

To improve an overall testing outlook, the following steps should be tried:
- Keeping in mind that the most reasonable expectation for taking a test is to expect to try to demonstrate as much of what you know as you possibly can.
- Reminding ourselves that a test is only one test; this is not the only one, and there will be others.
- The thought of thinking of oneself in an irrational, all-or-nothing term should be avoided at all costs.
- A reward should be designated for after the test, so there's something to look forward to. Whether it be going to a movie, going out to eat, or simply visiting friends, schedule it in advance, and do it no matter what result is expected on the exam.

Test-takers should also keep in mind that the basics are some of the most important things, even beyond anti-anxiety techniques and studying. Never neglect the basic social, emotional and biological needs, in order to try to absorb information. In order to best achieve, these three factors must be held as just as important as the studying itself.

Study Steps

Remember the following important steps for studying:
- Maintain healthy nutrition and exercise habits. Continue both your recreational activities and social pass times. These both contribute to your physical and emotional well being.
- Be certain to get a good amount of sleep, especially the night before the test, because when you're overtired you are not able to perform to the best of your best ability.
- Keep the studying pace to a moderate level by taking breaks when they are needed, and varying the work whenever possible, to keep the mind fresh instead of getting bored.

- When enough studying has been done that all the material that can be learned has been learned, and the test taker is prepared for the test, stop studying and do something relaxing such as listening to music, watching a movie, or taking a warm bubble bath.

There are also many other techniques to minimize the uneasiness or apprehension that is experienced along with test anxiety before, during, or even after the examination. In fact, there are a great deal of things that can be done to stop anxiety from interfering with lifestyle and performance. Again, remember that anxiety will not be eliminated entirely, and it shouldn't be. Otherwise that "up" feeling for exams would not exist, and most of us depend on that sensation to perform better than usual. However, this anxiety has to be at a level that is manageable.

Of course, as we have just discussed, being prepared for the exam is half the battle right away. Attending all classes, finding out what knowledge will be expected on the exam, and knowing the exam schedules are easy steps to lowering anxiety. Keeping up with work will remove the need to cram, and efficient study habits will eliminate wasted time. Studying should be done in an ideal location for concentration, so that it is simple to become interested in the material and give it complete attention. A method such as SQ3R (Survey, Question, Read, Recite, Review) is a wonderful key to follow to make sure that the study habits are as effective as possible, especially in the case of learning from a textbook. Flashcards are great techniques for memorization. Learning to take good notes will mean that notes will be full of useful information, so that less sifting will need to be done to seek out what is pertinent for studying. Reviewing notes after class and then again on occasion will keep the information fresh in the mind. From notes that have been taken summary sheets and outlines can be made for simpler reviewing.

A study group can also be a very motivational and helpful place to study, as there will be a sharing of ideas, all of the minds can work together, to make sure that everyone understands, and the studying will be made more interesting because it will be a social occasion.

Basically, though, as long as the test-taker remains organized and self confident, with efficient study habits, less time will need to be spent studying, and higher grades will be achieved.

To become self confident, there are many useful steps. The first of these is "self talk." It has been shown through extensive research, that self-talk for students who suffer from test anxiety, should be well monitored, in order to make sure that it contributes to self confidence as opposed to sinking the student. Frequently the self talk of test-anxious students is negative or self-defeating, thinking that everyone else is smarter and faster, that they always mess up, and that if they don't do well, they'll fail the entire course. It is important to decreasing anxiety that awareness is made of self talk. Try writing any negative self thoughts and then disputing them with a positive statement instead. Begin self-encouragement as though it was a friend speaking. Repeat positive statements to help reprogram the mind to believing in successes instead of failures.

Helpful Techniques

Other extremely helpful techniques include:
- Self-visualization of doing well and reaching goals
- While aiming for an "A" level of understanding, don't try to "overprotect" by setting your expectations lower. This will only convince the mind to stop studying in order to meet the lower expectations.
- Don't make comparisons with the results or habits of other students. These are individual factors, and different things work for different people, causing different results.
- Strive to become an expert in learning what works well, and what can be done in order to improve. Consider collecting this data in a journal.
- Create rewards for after studying instead of doing things before studying that will only turn into avoidance behaviors.
- Make a practice of relaxing - by using methods such as progressive relaxation, self-hypnosis, guided imagery, etc - in order to make relaxation an automatic sensation.
- Work on creating a state of relaxed concentration so that concentrating will take on the focus of the mind, so that none will be wasted on worrying.
- Take good care of the physical self by eating well and getting enough sleep.
- Plan in time for exercise and stick to this plan.

Beyond these techniques, there are other methods to be used before, during and after the test that will help the test-taker perform well in addition to overcoming anxiety.

Before the exam comes the academic preparation. This involves establishing a study schedule and beginning at least one week before the actual date of the test. By doing this, the anxiety of not having enough time to study for the test will be automatically eliminated. Moreover, this will make the studying a much more effective experience, ensuring that the learning will be an easier process. This relieves much undue pressure on the test-taker.

Summary sheets, note cards, and flash cards with the main concepts and examples of these main concepts should be prepared in advance of the actual studying time. A topic should never be eliminated from this process. By omitting a topic because it isn't expected to be on the test is only setting up the test-taker for anxiety should it actually appear on the exam. Utilize the course syllabus for laying out the topics that should be studied. Carefully go over the notes that were made in class, paying special attention to any of the issues that the professor took special care to emphasize while lecturing in class. In the textbooks, use the chapter review, or if possible, the chapter tests, to begin your review.

It may even be possible to ask the instructor what information will be covered on the exam, or what the format of the exam will be (for example, multiple choice, essay, free form, true-false). Additionally, see if it is possible to find out how many questions will be on the test. If a review sheet or sample test has been offered by the professor, make good use of it, above anything else, for the preparation for the test. Another great resource for getting to know the examination is reviewing tests from previous semesters. Use these tests to review, and aim to achieve a 100% score on each of the possible topics. With a few exceptions, the goal that you set for yourself is the highest one that you will reach.

Take all of the questions that were assigned as homework, and rework them to any other possible course material. The more problems reworked, the more skill and confidence will form as a result. When forming the solution to a problem, write out each of the steps. Don't simply do head work. By doing as many steps on paper as possible, much clarification and therefore confidence will be formed. Do this with as many homework problems as possible, before checking the answers. By checking the answer after each problem, a reinforcement will exist, that will not be on the exam. Study situations should be as exam-like as possible, to prime the test-taker's system for the experience. By waiting to check the answers at the end, a psychological advantage will be formed, to decrease the stress factor.

Another fantastic reason for not cramming is the avoidance of confusion in concepts, especially when it comes to mathematics. 8-10 hours of study will become one hundred percent more effective if it is spread out over a week or at least several days, instead of doing it all in one sitting. Recognize that the human brain requires time in order to assimilate new material, so frequent breaks and a span of study time over several days will be much more beneficial.

Additionally, don't study right up until the point of the exam. Studying should stop a minimum of one hour before the exam begins. This allows the brain to rest and put things in their proper order. This will also provide the time to become as relaxed as possible when going into the examination room. The test-taker will also have time to eat well and eat sensibly. Know that the brain needs food as much as the rest of the body. With enough food and enough sleep, as well as a relaxed attitude, the body and the mind are primed for success.

Avoid any anxious classmates who are talking about the exam. These students only spread anxiety, and are not worth sharing the anxious sentimentalities.

Before the test also involves creating a positive attitude, so mental preparation should also be a point of concentration. There are many keys to creating a positive attitude. Should fears become rushing in, make a visualization of taking the exam, doing well, and seeing an A written on the paper. Write out a list of affirmations that will bring a feeling of confidence, such as "I am doing well in my English class," "I studied well and know my material," "I enjoy this class." Even if the affirmations aren't believed at first, it sends a positive message to the subconscious which will result in an alteration of the overall belief system, which is the system that creates reality.

If a sensation of panic begins, work with the fear and imagine the very worst! Work through the entire scenario of not passing the test, failing the entire course, and dropping out of school, followed by not getting a job, and pushing a shopping cart through the dark alley where you'll live. This will place things into perspective! Then, practice deep breathing and create a visualization of the opposite situation - achieving an "A" on the exam, passing the entire course, receiving the degree at a graduation ceremony.

On the day of the test, there are many things to be done to ensure the best results, as well as the most calm outlook. The following stages are suggested in order to maximize test-taking potential:
- Begin the examination day with a moderate breakfast, and avoid any coffee or beverages with caffeine if the test taker is prone to jitters. Even people who are used to managing caffeine can feel jittery or light-headed when it is taken on a test day.
- Attempt to do something that is relaxing before the examination begins. As last minute cramming clouds the mastering of overall concepts, it is better to use this time to create a calming outlook.
- Be certain to arrive at the test location well in advance, in order to provide time to select a location that is away from doors, windows and other distractions, as well as giving enough time to relax before the test begins.
- Keep away from anxiety generating classmates who will upset the sensation of stability and relaxation that is being attempted before the exam.
- Should the waiting period before the exam begins cause anxiety, create a self-distraction by reading a light magazine or something else that is relaxing and simple.

During the exam itself, read the entire exam from beginning to end, and find out how much time should be allotted to each individual problem. Once writing the exam, should more time be taken for a problem, it should be abandoned, in order to begin another problem. If there is time at the end, the unfinished problem can always be returned to and completed.

Read the instructions very carefully - twice - so that unpleasant surprises won't follow during or after the exam has ended.

When writing the exam, pretend that the situation is actually simply the completion of homework within a library, or at home. This will assist in forming a relaxed atmosphere, and will allow the brain extra focus for the complex thinking function.

Begin the exam with all of the questions with which the most confidence is felt. This will build the confidence level regarding the entire exam and will begin a quality momentum. This will also create encouragement for trying the problems where uncertainty resides.

Going with the "gut instinct" is always the way to go when solving a problem. Second guessing should be avoided at all costs. Have confidence in the ability to do well.

For essay questions, create an outline in advance that will keep the mind organized and make certain that all of the points are remembered. For multiple choice, read every answer, even if the correct one has been spotted - a better one may exist.

Continue at a pace that is reasonable and not rushed, in order to be able to work carefully. Provide enough time to go over the answers at the end, to check for small errors that can be corrected.

Should a feeling of panic begin, breathe deeply, and think of the feeling of the body releasing sand through its pores. Visualize a calm, peaceful place, and include all of the sights, sounds and sensations of this image. Continue the deep breathing, and take a few minutes to continue this with closed eyes. When all is well again, return to the test.

If a "blanking" occurs for a certain question, skip it and move on to the next question. There will be time to return to the other question later. Get everything done that can be done, first, to guarantee all the grades that can be compiled, and to build all of the confidence possible. Then return to the weaker questions to build the marks from there.

Remember, one's own reality can be created, so as long as the belief is there, success will follow. And remember: anxiety can happen later, right now, there's an exam to be written!

After the examination is complete, whether there is a feeling for a good grade or a bad grade, don't dwell on the exam, and be certain to follow through on the reward that was promised...and enjoy it! Don't dwell on any mistakes that have been made, as there is nothing that can be done at this point anyway. Additionally, don't begin to study for the next test right away. Do something relaxing for a while, and let the mind relax and prepare itself to begin absorbing information again.

From the results of the exam - both the grade and the entire experience, be certain to learn from what has gone on. Perfect studying habits and work some more on confidence in order to make the next examination experience even better than the last one.

Learn to avoid places where openings occurred for laziness, procrastination and day dreaming.

Use the time between this exam and the next one to better learn to relax, even learning to relax on cue, so that any anxiety can be controlled during the next exam. Learn how to relax the body. Slouch in your chair if that helps. Tighten and then relax all of the different muscle groups, one group at a time, beginning with the feet and then working all the way up to the neck and face. This will ultimately relax the muscles more than they were to begin with. Learn how to breathe deeply and comfortably, and focus on this breathing going in and out as a relaxing thought. With every exhale, repeat the word "relax."

As common as test anxiety is, it is very possible to overcome it. Make yourself one of the test-takers who overcome this frustrating hindrance.

Additional Bonus Material

Due to our efforts to try to keep this book to a manageable length, we've created a link that will give you access to all of your additional bonus material.

Please visit http://www.mometrix.com/bonus948/vsolg8read to access the information.